We Were There

We Were There

Revelations from the Dallas Doctors Who Attended to JFK on November 22, 1963

ALLEN CHILDS, MD

SKYHORSE PUBLISHING

Skyhorse Publishing books may be purchased in bulk at special discounts for sales promotion, corporate gifts, fund-raising, or educational purposes. Special editions can also be created to specifications. For details, contact the Special Sales Department, Skyhorse Publishing, 307 West 36th Street, 11th Floor, New York, NY 10018 or info@skyhorsepublishing.com.

Skyhorse® and Skyhorse Publishing® are registered trademarks of Skyhorse Publishing, Inc.®, a Delaware corporation.

Visit our website at www.skyhorsepublishing.com.

10 9 8 7 6 5 4 3 2 1

Library of Congress Cataloging-in-Publication Data is available on file.

ISBN: 978-1-62636-108-9

Printed in the United States

For my loving grandchildren, Jackson Childs, Joshua Morgan, Stephanie Klarer, Erin Elizabeth, and Jacob Newton, Natalie Sunstrum Fellows, and Nicole and Aaron Mason Sunstrum.

CONTENTS

ACKNOWLEDGMENTS

Not a story would have been collected without the efforts of the UT Southwestern Alumni Association's Julie Mages and director Wes Norred, who graciously sent out my request for memories of that November day. The collection became a book after a chance encounter over a lox and bagel brunch with Ambassador Stuart Eizenstat. He took the initiative to send the manuscript to his long time literary agent, the author and attorney, Ron Goldfarb. Ron worked for Robert Kennedy and was in his office when the news of the assassination reached them.

Hope Eastman provided sustained and invaluable help in the preparation of this book, particularly with her insightful thematic suggestions. I am grateful for the artful editorial changes made by Holly Rubino, my editor at Skyhorse Publishing.

And, to my co-authors, I thank you for the thoughtful, often touching memories you sent me. Looking back through the corridors of time, you have preserved for all time the historical fabric of that day at Parkland, half a century ago.

INTRODUCTION

Twice in a forty-five hour, thirty-one minute timeframe, Parkland Hospital was the center of worldwide attention. It was the temporary seat of the United States government, as well as the state of Texas. Our thirty-fifth president died in Trauma Room 1. At that moment, the ascendency of the thirty-sixth president of the United States occurred at Parkland. Two days later, it was the site of death of the president's accused assassin. So reported a Parkland Hospital office memorandum dated November 27, 1963.

And *we were there*.

We forty-five physician alumni of Southwestern Medical School reached back nearly five decades and found the branding iron memories of November 22, 1963. It began at the forty-fifth reunion of the class of 1966. During our dinner meeting, twenty-four doctors and their significant others told stories for two hours, including fond memories of classmates who were no longer with us. Perhaps that grief led us to remember another sadness. First a trickle, then a flood of memories of that devastating day reawakened our common bond of that experience. Our classmate Kaye Wilkins said, "We ought to record these memories for posterity." As class president, I agreed to collect and publish these recollections. I wrote a letter which the Alumni Association mailed to every student, intern, and resident who was at Parkland and Southwestern the day President John F. Kennedy died in Trauma Room 1.

Like the patrons of Ford's Theater who witnessed the assassination of President Lincoln, a blood spattered history had assaulted our senses. Some of us were in the emergency operating room, some in the hallway of the "pit," and others stood a stricken vigil at the ER loading dock. So many of the main participants have died—Dr. M. T. "Pepper" Jenkins, the chief of anesthesiology, and surgeons Charles Baxter, Malcolm Perry, and alas, the first doctor to reach the dying president, Jim Carrico. I have included their own words from the oral history collections of the Sixth Floor Museum, which is in the Dallas County Administration Building (formerly the Texas School Book Depository).

Earl Rose, who was a forensic pathologist and the Dallas County Medical Examiner at the time, spoke out forcefully against the conspiracy theorists. He was the one who stood in the path of Secret Service agents who were breaking the law by removing the president's body from Parkland.

In putting together this book, I was helped greatly by two surgeons in Trauma Room 1, Doctors Ron Jones and Robert McClelland. Jones did a cutdown on President Kennedy's left arm, established an intravenous line in less than a minute, and also inserted a chest tube. He is now Chief of Surgery at Baylor Hospital, and he kindly sent me his memories as published in *Baylor Reflections*. Robert McClelland is, at age eighty-four, still teaching surgery at Southwestern. McClelland stood at the head of the table on which the dying president lay, and held a retractor for Doctors Baxter and Perry who were performing a tracheotomy. He told me to quote from an article published in *D Magazine* in 2008, in which he detailed his memories of not only the final moments of the president's life, but also his own participation in the emergency surgery of Lee Harvey Oswald. McClelland's oral history from the Sixth Floor Museum is particularly compelling.

Conspiracy theories have continued to rage for fifty years since that day, and were not put to rest by the Warren Commission's conclusion that there was a single shooter and a single bullet that killed President Kennedy and injured Governor Connally. The doctors at Parkland were the only ones who saw the neck wound before the emergency tracheotomy, and they were unanimous that the neck wound was an entry wound. In time, most, but not all, no longer would believe this.

Late in this project, I came upon a startling revelation in Dr. Ron Jones's oral history. After taking his Warren Commission deposition at Parkland, chief counsel Arlen Specter told Jones, "We have people who would testify that they saw somebody shoot the president from the front. But we don't want to interview them, and I don't want you saying anything about that, either."

Senior Chest Surgery Resident James "Red" Duke was in charge of Governor Connally's emergency care, after a brief encounter with the scene in Trauma Room 1. A bullet had punctured the Governor's lung and shattered his wrist. A senior medical student, Bill Scroggie, had stumbled on the Governor unattended because all the attention was on the president. Scroggie, observing Connally's respiratory distress, grabbed Duke, whose immediate intervention saved the Governor's life. The living was almost lost in the struggle to save the dead.

One of the more curious phenomena is how people's memories were clear to them but conflicted with others. One is what Kemp Clark, the chief of neurosurgery, was reported to have said before he pronounced the president dead. Also, where he was before he was summoned to the ER is variously remembered. Because of his name, the students referred to Kemp Clark as "man super" Dr. Clark, a tall, trim, and mildly aloof professor of neurosurgery, told the Warren Commission that he was summoned from his laboratory by a phone call. Some students recall that he was giving a lecture to med students in the school's auditorium. I and my medical school roommate, Dr. Rick Cohen, recall seeing him in the Parkland library, from which he hurried out after someone ran in to tell him something. The overhead pages for department chairmen to report to the ER began to blare just after that.

A rich vein of recollection is reported from those of us who stood at the ER loading dock, before and after being herded back behind police barricades. We looked into the presidential limousine with its top down and saw the back seat covered in blood and the roses on the floor. There were about a hundred and fifty of us standing there when we received word that the president had died, about a half an hour before it was announced to the world. I think it was Kemp Clark who told some of the students as he was walking out of the ER. I can never forget how the wailing of the black people contrasted with the stunned, but dry-eyed silence of the medical students. Dr. Robert Duchouquette sent me his narrative poem which begins, "The whole nation cried the day I met JFK."

Yet, as I record in chapter 12, not everyone was sorrowful that sad November day. Rick Cohen reminded me that when he and I went back over to the school, some of our classmates were actually *celebrating*. I wish he hadn't. *None* of them sent their memories to me. Particularly disturbing was Dr. Al Lindsey's recollection of a fifth-grade class cheering when their tearful teacher told them the president had died. This was by no means confined to Dallas, but Lindsey recalled a prominent local minister saying, "The only thing worse than the assassination would be for Dallas not to acknowledge that it was a city full of hatred, a perfect environment for such an event to take place."

As the fiftieth anniversary of the assassination nears, articles have appeared such as Ross Douthat's *New York Times* op-ed, "The Enduring Cult of Kennedy," printed on November 27, 2011. In the article, Douthat commented, "No matter how many times the myths of Camelot are seemingly interred by history, they always come shambling back to life—in another television special, another *Vanity Fair* cover, another hardcover. . . ." The same can be said for conspiracy theories that do not loosen their grip on the public imagination. It is said that a thousand books have been published on the assassination. Among the "myths" the *Times* article explored is the conviction that JFK was a martyr to right-wing unreason. How *can* that notion square with the fact that Oswald was a leftist pro-Castro agitator whose other assassination target was the right-wing segregationist, General Edwin Walker?

Adlai Stevenson II, when he was the US Ambassador to the United Nations, had tried to discourage JFK's visit to Dallas. Stevenson had been spat upon and struck with a placard during his most recent public appearance there because of his political views. But, Vice President Lyndon Johnson prevailed upon the president to visit Dallas where his mission was to patch up some tattered alliances between fellow democrats: the conservative governor, John Connally, and the widely admired liberal senator, Ralph Yarborough.

President and Mrs. Kennedy were greeted by an exuberant crowd at Love Field, and they looked happily immersed in it. My classmate David Haymes was so close he could take pictures of them in the crowd and riding in the limousine. The next he and fellow classmate Cervando Martinez saw of them, the presidential limousine was racing frantically, a Secret Service agent clinging precariously to the trunk. As the motorcade careened by, they saw Jackie covered with blood, shielding the president's head in her lap.

After the president was loaded onto a gurney, a wall of people entered the emergency room. His head was covered by two dozen roses, and he was noted to be motionless and mannequin-like as they rushed him into Trauma Room 1.

First year student, Larry Dossey, held the telephone line open to CBS in New York City for their reporter, Robert Pierpoint. As this was long before cell or satellite phones, the pay phones in the ER were few and the only way to contact the outside world. For more than an hour, Dossey guarded the open line, and described to CBS what he was seeing in the ER, while Pierpoint went back and forth to Trauma Room 1. When Pierpoint told Walter Cronkite, who was broadcasting live, that the priests had administered the Last Rites to the president, Cronkite would then say, "I guess it doesn't get any more official than that."

Abram "Chic" Eisenstein, another medical student, saw the Secret Service commandeer a car to whisk away Lyndon Johnson. A Mexican-American man pulled up to the loading dock of the ER with his very soon-to-deliver wife, and the Secret Service allowed them in but stole their car.

Many of us saw President Johnson, ghostly pale, surrounded by a ring of Secret Service men trundling him into that car. The delay in announcing JFK's death was said to allow President Johnson time to get to Love Field, where he was to be sworn in aboard Air Force One. This delay was the first order issued by the new president, immediately after Assistant White House Press Secretary Malcolm Kilduff was the first to address LBJ as "Mr. President."

And then those of us standing on the perimeter of the loading dock saw the bronze casket placed into the white hearse, and the former First Lady, her pink Chanel suit vividly stained with her husband's blood, get in with the casket.

Memories of Jackie Kennedy are in many of the narratives I received, and they reflect a primal sympathy for her. I have also included statements from Pepper Jenkins, the anesthesia chief, who said, "As she circled and circled, I noticed her hands were cupped in front of her, as if she were cradling something. As she passed, she nudged me with an elbow and handed me what she had been nursing with her hands—a large chunk of her husband's brain tissue." Christie Jenkins, the daughter of Dr. M. T. Pepper Jenkins (the anesthesiologist on the resuscitation team) has confirmed that Mrs. Kennedy nudged her father and handed him pieces of the president's brain that she'd been holding. One of the most touching memories of the First Lady is from Adel Nafrawi, a surgery resident, who witnessed Jackie move toward the dead president, remove the wedding ring from his hand, kiss him, and put the ring on her finger.

After Last Rites were administered, the Secret Service agents were struggling for control of the chaotic emergency room. Senior medical student Bill Scroggie noted, "There was a well-dressed man guarding the back door of the ER and another fellow tries to push his way through without identifying himself. The Secret Service agent flattened the guy. I later learned he was an FBI agent." Then there was the historic confrontation in Trauma Room 1 between Dallas County Medical Examiner, Earl Rose, and the Secret Service over the custody of the president's mortal remains. In addition to being a notable forensic pathologist, Rose held a law degree, and he challenged the legal authority of the Secret Service to remove the body. Many subsequent conspiracy theories center on the broken chain of evidence born of this confrontation. An article published in 1992 in the *Journal of the American Medical Association* quotes Rose as saying, ". . . I was in their way. I was face-to-face with Secret Service agent Roy H. Kellerman, and I was trying to explain to him that Texas law applied in the instant case of the death of the president, and that the law required an autopsy to be performed in Texas."

"No one was in charge of the situation," Rose continued. "Agent Kellerman tried three tactics to have his way—he asserted his identity as representing the Secret Service; he appealed for sympathy to Mrs. Kennedy; and he used body language to attempt to bully, or should I say, intimidate. . . . At no time did I feel I was in physical danger because he and the others were armed. I was not looking at Agent Kellerman's gun, I was looking at his eyes, and they were very intense. His eyes said he meant to get the president's body back to Washington."

In the wrung-out silence of the Parkland ER, after President Johnson, Jackie Kennedy, and the bronze casket had gone, Doctors Michael Ellsasser and Don Gilliard walked into Trauma Room 1 before it was cleaned. In a waste basket they found the two dozen red roses given to the First Lady at Love Field that morning. Each removed a single rose. Ellsasser preserved his and has kept it to this day.

Like President Lincoln's box at the Ford's Theatre, the Parkland emergency operating room is lock-stitched into the fabric of history, preserved at the request of the Kennedy family. In 1973, the federal government purchased all of the equipment in Trauma Room 1 and it is now housed in the National Archives underground facility at Lenexa, Kansas. Many of the medical staff have their own mementos of that day. Robert McClelland still has the bloody shirt he wore while he cared for the dying president.

Things were different when Lee Harvey Oswald was shot forty-eight hours later. Seeing a prostrate Oswald on his home TV, McClelland rushed to Parkland, where he encountered surgery chairman, Tom Shires, who was going home after tending to his post-operative patient, Governor Connally. McClelland flashed his headlights and when Shires pulled over, he told him what had happened to Oswald. Unlike with President Kennedy, McClelland had time to change into his scrubs before operating.

Already deeply unsettled by the events two days prior, twenty-five million viewers recoiled in horror at the sight of Jack Ruby firing point blank at Oswald's abdomen. At that moment, it did not seem to matter that he was the most hated man in the world. Minutes after this first televised assassination, a moribund and unconscious Oswald—"white as a piece of paper," said McClelland—made it to the Parkland ER, accompanied by Secret Service agents. Dr. Harry Eastman, on duty in the psychiatry section, recalls, "Suddenly all doors were sealed with men in suits with machine guns drawn." One was to stand by in case Oswald wished to make a death-bed confession. In his last conscious act, Oswald had declined to say anything when told by a sheriff at the jail that he was gravely injured.

Once again, the earth shook and Parkland was at the epicenter. Ron Jones, chief surgery resident, Malcolm Perry, Shires and McClelland operated for more than an hour, administering sixteen pints of blood, before Oswald's heart arrested. Perry opened his chest and in a final desperate effort, began open cardiac massage to no avail.

The following eyewitness memories gathered here paint a previously unseen tapestry of this unforgettable time. Some recollections are like the grainy black and white TV pictures of the day, but many more are the graphic technicolor of surreal dreams. The chapters that follow detail the sights and feelings of our forty-five authors when the shock wave hit first Parkland Hospital, and then the world. Their immediate actions, what they saw and felt are vividly remembered herein, half a century from that fateful November day.

CHAPTER 1

WRITTEN AT THE TIME, REMEMBERED FOR ALL TIME

"I just came from Parkland and I wanted to write this while I remember how it really is," wrote Kenneth Farrimond to his girlfriend, Susan. His freshman medical school classmate, Jed Rosenthal, began his letter, "Ma—Enclosed is an account of what happened today. . . . I was there—I felt him die." Dudley Jones, another medical student, ended his letter to his folks with what we all thought, "It is still hard for one to comprehend, that such could happen in 1963."

These three young men had a sense of their own history, and sufficient maturity to pull themselves together enough to communicate eloquently with their loved ones. Their letters are reproduced in this chapter in their entirety, and, as with most other of the forty eyewitness reports, parts of them appear in other chapters as well. I thank Farrimond, Rosenthal, and Jones for their thoughtfulness in sharing them with posterity.

An original copy of the *Parkland Papers* of November 1963, which contains the remarkable office memorandum written a few days after the assassination (and also reproduced here in its entirety), was sent to me by Charles Raney. He was kind enough to give me his perfectly preserved copy of the *Dallas Morning News* published twenty-five years after that fateful November day.

JED ROSENTHAL, MD

Friday, November 22, 1963

Ma—

Enclosed is an account of what happened today. The way I saw it and the way I feel about it. I would like to keep this letter. I am writing it now because I know I will not be able to express how it affected me later on. I only wish I could write better and therefore express more correctly my feelings. This has upset me and angered me considerably. I am just going to let my mind go on paper.

Sorry I won't be there for Thanksgiving—I shall really miss it. So long for now.

Love, Jed

> *Dallas, Texas, November 22, 1963*
> *I still cannot believe what has happened today. The president of the United States, the leader of our country, the symbol of freedom to the world has been shot down— is dead—murdered.*
> *Had I not been in Dallas at Parkland Hospital where he died, I do not think that I would realize what*

has happened. But I was there—I felt him die. I can think of only one other time when I was so emotionally upset—the day Dad died.

Ace, Kenneth, Fritz Barton, and Hank Bradley, all students at Southwestern Medical Center, were sitting in the apartment discussing radical groups in the United States. The John Birch Society was under fire—whether or not it is basically a group of patriotic people who have attracted a radical following, or is it in essence a radical dangerous group. We had discussed General Edwin Walker's activities. All of us thought that he would be under heavy surveillance today while the president was in Dallas. All of us, though not agreeing with the president's domestic policies, did agree that no one should picket his visit to Dallas, or in any way embarrass him by demonstrations or jeers during his stay here. He is the leader of our country and should be treated with the greatest respect. If you do not agree with his points of view, fine. Support and vote for someone else—but don't degrade the president. I repeat we all felt very strongly about this. We were all hoping that we would get to see the president as he passed by the medical school on his way to Love Field.

It was now around 12:45. We were getting ready to go back to school. John Carnet (another student) came in and shouted, "The president has been shot! He is being taken to Parkland Hospital." We could tell by the look on his face that this unfortunately was not a bad joke. Kenneth and I raced to his car (I didn't notice where the others were) and started for school. On the way out I noticed Maurice, the colored cook at the Phi Chi house, standing by the stairs crying. I knew now that the report was true—that President Kennedy had been shot.

Kenneth and I reached school within five minutes, parked the car and ran over to the emergency exit at Parkland. The president, along with Governor John Connally, had just been taken into the hospital. By this time about 150 people had gathered outside the emergency room. The car in which the presidential party had been riding was by the loading dock. The bouquet of roses that Mrs. Kennedy had received was lying on the blood-stained floor of the special Continental convertible, whose bubble top had not been used because the president didn't think it necessary—it was too fine a day!

The crowd had heard no news as to the condition of the president or governor. It was rumored that the president had been shot in the head. The faces of the crowd were confused, worried, some tear-stained. Everyone was saying some type of prayer.

A police car arrived and two large cartons marked "human blood" were carried into the hospital. About this same time two priests entered the hospital. There still was no news. A while later the priests came out. Reporters swarmed around them. They gave no news, but it was evident that last rites had been administered and our president was dying. However, there was no definite news and therefore still rays of hope. These were soon crushed when a man (presumably a doctor) announced that the president of the United States was dead. The time, a little after 1:00 p.m.

Some people started crying and sobbing uncontrollably—others like myself just stood there dazed, fighting back the tears. No one moved for a minute or so. Then cameras started snapping all around and reporters began questioning members of the presidential motorcade. It was a scene of confusion and disbelief. People were in fact questioning if this all was really happening or was it just a horrible dream, or imagination. These questions were soon answered as a hearse pulled up and a large ornate bronze-colored casket was carried into the hospital.

Lyndon Johnson and his wife came out of the emergency room door surrounded by Secret Service men. They were rushed into a waiting car. We later learned that the car drove immediately to Love Field and the presidential jet. Lyndon Johnson was met there by Sarah T. Hughes, a federal district judge, and Mr. Johnson was sworn in as president. The great plane that brought one president to Texas was to take a different president back to Washington.

Mrs. Kennedy and the body of her husband were still in the hospital. The crowd was waiting for her to come out with the casket containing the president's body. I had no desire to see Mrs. Kennedy at this terrible time. I think grief is a very private, personal thing. Kenneth, Ace and I went back to the apartment and started to watch the endless newscasts. No one said very much.

I cannot believe that there could be in this, the most wonderful nation that has ever existed, a person so twisted in mind and spirit that he could commit this hideous crime. It is indeed a black, black day.

It is hard to believe that this man who earlier this morning was in such good spirits and health no longer lives, that he was dastardly shot down in the physical, mental and political prime of his life. Only last week I very much enjoyed the so human pictures of him and little John in Look magazine.

The government of the United States will not slow down. Tomorrow will come and other tomorrows will follow it. There is already a new president, the 36th, Lyndon Johnson. I have great faith in President Johnson. I believe that as president he will give our country the same excellent leadership he did as Majority Leader of the Senate. I am sure right now the country is earnestly behind him. The entire world is shocked and is looking at America to see what will happen. This is a grave and serious time, but I am sure that President Johnson will rise to the occasion. We will show the world again what "kind of stuff" American people are made of.

Now all the people of these United States are united regardless of race, color or creed in a common grief. I only hope that when this grief wears off, the common union of all men will remain.

Jed

Nov. 23, 1963
1 day after

Dear Folks,

It was a dreary Friday morning. The skies were fullof moisture- drissly type with a little rain here and there. I wasn't really thinking about much except my oral quiz that I had scheduled around 1 o'clock in Pediatrics over at the Med School that day. I had a conference at Parkland at 9:15 and it wasstill ~~still~~ messy. I just decided I would stay at the school and study there instead of going back to Texas Childrens Hosp. I came out of the library to go over to Parkland to eat lunch and the skies were almost completely clear with a nice cool northern breeze pushing the heavy clouds southward. The skies were a beautiful blue and soon there was not a cloud left in sight. I phoned A.L. to see if she had noted how beautiful it had become since 10:30 and made her get the mail and see how pretty it had gotten. We couldn't beleeved it had changed so rapidly. I ate and returned to the school library to get my last minute study- ing in before my quiz . This was around 12 noon. Sitting one table down from me was one of the Parkland Staff surgeons reading. At approx. 12:40, one of the librarians came rushing over to the surgeon saying that he was needed immediately at the emergency room because the President had been shot. His reply, "aw your kidding"- I imagine all of our first replies. But as we all so ~~XXX~~ shookingly know- it was true! As you can imagine my quiz was canceled. In disbelief, I went upstairs to where my quiz was to be.There I listened to the radio and looked out the window towards the E.R. were the President lies. I walked over towards the emergency room(E.R.)- not so much as a curiosity seeker but as many- disbelief that The President of the U.S. was dying inside from a mortal wound- here in Dallas - in 1963 in these our United States.

There is no doubt in my mind that the President died immediately from the description that was given me and he was dead on arrival at Parkland. I did get a glimpse at the new President and his wife as they left the sceneand later saw the former President leave in the Hearst for Love Field. As for the Gov.- he is doing fine and will completely recover unless infection complicates the matter. Fate was on the Gov. side in his case- Parkland deals with gunshot wounds in the chest daily and he couldn't have been in better surgical hands than Dr. Shaw's. The rest- you know.

It is still hard for one to comprehend- that such could happen in 1963.

Love *Dudley*
Dudley

3322 Daniels
Dallas 5, Texas

The day President Kennedy
was ~~assassinated~~
Nov 22, 1963

Mrs Maud M. Jones
2129 W. Mulberry
San Antonio 1, Texas

DALLAS, TEX.
10 00 AM
25 NOV
1963

5¢
U

KENNETH FARRIMOND, MD

(his letter to his girlfriend, Susan)

November 22, 1963

Dear Susan,

I just came from Parkland and I wanted to write this while I remember how it really is.

At noon a bunch of us were talking politics here in the apartment when John Carnet [class of '67 who dropped out after freshman year] came in and said the president had been shot and taken to Parkland Hospital. I didn't really believe it—still don't—not today, not in Dallas. John, Jed [Rosenthal '67], Ace [Wallace Moore '67] and I went immediately to the school and walked over to the hospital emergency entrance.

His car was still there—with blood stains on the back seat and Jackie's bouquet of yellow roses on the floor. The confusion was unreal. Not many people, but nobody knew anything except that he was shot. A doctor or intern that one boy knew came out a backdoor and told us there was no hope—that he was dying fast.

By this time people had gathered. Sen. Yarborough stood near us crying and talking to the press. He kept saying "it was terrible." Police and secret service people were all over the place but they didn't seem to know what to do. We could go anyplace.

People from the motorcade were all over the place, and everybody's story was different—except all had heard three shots. Everyone, police included, milled around like lost animals awaiting a slaughter. Over and over I heard "God damn!" or "My God!" or just simply "No!" Stories ranged from "dead-on-arrival" to "slightly wounded." We knew more than anyone. Then a loud speaker said from somewhere, "The president is dead."

Some people cried but most looked like they still couldn't believe it—I know I couldn't. A minute later a big off-white Cadillac hearse pulled up with what appeared to be a huge bronze casket in the back.

All this time I had been sort of wandering around. I happened back upon the doctor from the emergency room. He was saying that apparently one shot had entered the back of Kennedy's head and got out the front of his neck. From the position of the entry wound brain damage must have been gigantic. Bleeding was profuse. They did a tracheotomy immediately and gave oxygen and blood—but no luck. The president died right there in the emergency room where I've worked on people myself, and Connally was taken straight to the trauma surgery since his wound wasn't so bad.

People began wandering off like stray cattle. A minute later L.B.J. came out surrounded by secret service men and rushed off in a Ford. He was white as a ghost and a couple of the secret service men were holding him up it looked like. Then the crowd really began to leave.

John Hugh, another freshman, came up—he was really shook. He'd just finished eating lunch at the hospital and was coming through the emergency room when the president's car drove up. He watched them unload the body and take it into the pit (emergency room operating theaters). He said that the president had his head on Jackie's lap when the car arrived. He was unconscious and covered with blood, as was his wife. They put him on a wheeled stretcher and took him to the pit with Jackie walking along beside him. She was very calm. That's all he saw. Then the police moved the crowd back.

We left a minute later, but Hank [Bradley '67] stayed and watched the hearse leave with the body and Mrs. Kennedy. She had on a pink dress, he said, and no hat. She was calm in appearance.

That's all I remember except for seeing the priests go in and then come back out later. Maybe it's not all in order, but I'm kind of confused at the moment.

I didn't agree with his politics, but he was the president. And it's such a pretty day. Too pretty to die on.

Everyone else is watching the TV reports. I think I'll join them.

Love,
Kenneth

P.S. Save this. I might want to read it after I get events sorted out.
—K

DALLAS COUNTY HOSPITAL DISTRICT

Office Memorandum
November 27, 1963

To: All Employees

At 12:38 p.m., Friday, November 22, 1963, President John F. Kennedy
and Texas' Governor John Connally were brought to the Emergency Room of
Parkland Memorial Hospital after being struck down by the bullets of an
assassin.

At 1:07 p.m., Sunday, November 24, 1963, Lee H. Oswald, accused
assassin of the late president, died in an operating room of Parkland
Memorial Hospital after being shot by a bystander in the basement of
Dallas' City Hall. In the intervening 48 hours and 31 minutes Parkland
Memorial Hospital had:

1. Become the temporary seat of the government of the United States.

2. Become the temporary seat of the government of the State of Texas.

3. Become the site of the death of the 35th President.

4. Become the site of the ascendency of the 36th President.

5. Become site of the death of President Kennedy's accused assassin.

6. Twice become the center of the attention of the world.

7. Continued to function at close to normal pace as a large
   charity hospital.

What is it that enables an institution to take in stride such a
series of history jolting events? Spirit? Dedication? Preparedness?
Certainly, all of these are important, but the underlying factor is
people. People whose education and training is sound. People whose
judgment is calm and perceptive. People whose actions are deliberate
and definitive. Our pride is not that we were swept up by the whirlwind
of tragic history, but that when we were, we were not found wanting.

C. J. Price
Administrator

CHAPTER 2

LOVE FIELD AND THE TRADE MART

The dreary clouds had lifted by the time Air Force One touched down at Love Field a mile from the medical school. My classmates, Al Lindsey, Cervando Martinez, David Haymes, and Wayne Mathews, played hooky from class and crowded into the airport to greet the president and the First Lady.

Vice President Johnson had prevailed on JFK to visit Dallas to do a bit of pre-election fence mending, as the conservative Governor John Connally and liberal senator Ralph Yarborough were at odds. Surely Kennedy's charm could smooth this over.

My classmates were a few feet away from the president and Jackie, close enough for David Haymes to take pictures of an obviously happy couple surrounded by an exuberant crowd, and again as they pulled away in the open top limousine. The removal of the bubble top from the limousine for the unseasonably warm day doomed the president.

The first stop for the motorcade, which included both Senator Yarborough and Governor Connally, was to be a luncheon speech at the Trade Mart. Awaiting his arrival were senior medical student Leslie Moore and his wife, who had been invited to the large gathering. The salads had already been served when Moore saw TV cameramen and reporters suddenly huddle around a walkie-talkie device.

Martinez and Haymes had driven from Love Field to the Trade Mart to get another glimpse of the president. When word shot through the crowd that "something had happened," they quickly climbed up a highway ramp sign beside the freeway. They heard sirens and saw the blur of the presidential limousine as it raced by, a blood-covered Jackie cradling the head of her mortally wounded husband and the Secret Service agent clinging to the trunk.

Courtesy of David Haymes, MD

Upraised hands greet our First Lady as she appears at the door of Air Force One.

DAVID HAYMES, MD

Friday, November 22 was clear but cooler as the four of us decided to miss class and head to Love Field to welcome President and Mrs. Kennedy. I think we took my car but can't be sure. Cervando Martinez, Wayne Mathews, Charlie Briseno, and I found places probably four or five people deep in the crowd on the tarmac where Air Force One was to arrive. We watched excitedly as it touched down and taxied in front of us. And then suddenly, the door opened and there they were! Jack and Jackie, smiling, waving, charismatic even from a distance. They descended the steps and immediately moved to embrace the crowd. I held my camera over my head and snapped away. (I still regret to this day that the pictures are not better!) We were enthralled to be this close and as they moved toward the limousine, I raced to the road where I guessed they would exit. Sure enough they passed about ten yards from me and I got a shot that, while blurry, leaves no doubt who the subjects are.

AL LINDSEY, MD

My decision to go see Air Force One land that day in Dallas was a spur-of-the moment thing. Since I was cutting microbiology class, I felt a little guilty about it, and I don't believe I even thought of asking anyone to go with me. But I got to Love Field and saw the planes land and thought they were beautiful.

Courtesy of the Dallas Morning News

The president and First Lady Jackie stepped off Air Force One into an exuberant crowd gathered on the tarmac of Love Field. Vice President Johnson and Ladybird beam in the background. Behind them is a somber Governor John Connally, soon to be thrust onto center stage of this historic day.

CERVANDO MARTINEZ, MD

The next morning David Haymes and I, and maybe others, I don't recall, skipped class (I think we "skipped" class, we may have had no classes) and drove to Love Field to see his arrival. David owned a camera and took some great shots of JFK up close on foot and then in the car.

Courtesy of David Haymes, MD

The joyous crowd on the tarmac soon engulfed our president and First Lady.

Courtesy of David Haymes, MD

A gracious Jackie Kennedy reaches out to well wishers.

Mrs. Kennedy approaches the limousine through an adoring throng.

Courtesy of David Haymes, MD

No one stood between David Haymes and the presidential motorcade as it pulled away from a cheering crowd.

Courtesy of David Haymes, MD

Courtesy of David Haymes, MD

Still on the tarmac at Love Field, my classmate David Haymes ran to a vantage point in time to photograph the president and Governor Connally sweep by en route to the tragedy only a few minutes away. As the motorcade turned the corner of Houston and Elm, the cheering along the parade route caused Nellie Connally to exclaim, "Mr. Kennedy, you can't say Dallas doesn't love you!" These were the last words President John F. Kennedy would ever hear.

LESLIE MOORE, MD

I was a senior medical student and my wife and I had been invited to the luncheon at the Dallas Trade Mart to hear the president speak. The arrival of President Kennedy was to be at noon. The first course was served at our table, but each of us refused to eat before the guest of honor had arrived. At about 12:10 or so, the guests at most tables were getting restless in a nervous sense, not an impatient sense. I saw a group of TV cameramen and reporters huddled around a walkie-talkie like device not more than fifteen or twenty-nine feet away. So I got up from my table and asked what was going on and they said, "The president has been shot."

If the answer was accurate, I knew they would be taking him to Parkland, so my wife and I got up from our table and headed out an exit door. No one else was visible in the parking lot, all seemed to have remained inside the building. We jumped in my VW Beetle and headed over to Parkland.

CERVANDO MARTINEZ, MD

We drove to the Trade Mart, parked the car, and while going to position ourselves where we could see him again, we heard the first news that something had happened. I don't recall that we knew what the "something" was, so we climbed on a highway ramp sign and soon heard sirens and saw the blur of the presidential car go by. I vividly remember seeing a man clinging to the back bumper reaching forward and the pink of Jackie's dress draped over JFK. We then realized what had happened, that he was shot. The word may have also been in the crowd by then, I don't know.

DAVID HAYMES, MD

We then returned to our car and cut across town to the Merchandise Mart on Stemmons Expressway while the motorcade wound its way through downtown. We parked near Harry Hines and walked to Stemmons and stood next to a telephone pole in front of the Merchandise Mart that still stands. As the motorcade approached we waved in anticipation. The motorcade didn't slow and sped past us allowing only a glimpse of the limousine. Over the years what we saw and what we think we saw, have become inseparably mixed. I've always told people that we saw the president after he had been shot and Jackie hovering over him but I can't be sure. All we knew was that something untoward had happened, possibly that someone had gotten sick. As we raced to our car we asked a motorcycle officer what had happened and he said he didn't know but the motorcade was going to Parkland Hospital. So we drove to Parkland (I have no idea where we parked) and headed to the emergency room but were barred from entering so we raced up stairs to try another entry point and that's when we heard. We passed a nurse on the stairs who said so clinically, "Kennedy's dead and they're taking Connally to surgery." We gave up our mission and gathered in front of the emergency room with all the other stunned students, faculty, police, and citizens. I don't remember much about the day after that.

CHAPTER 3

PARKLAND AND SOUTHWESTERN

It was Friday, and the weekly internal medicine death conference on Parkland's sixth floor was winding down toward a merciful end. As always, *whose* death it was depended on which intern or resident's case had been selected for laser dissection by Donald Seldin, chairman of internal medicine. Arguably one of the world's greatest teachers of medicine, his ferocity and inquisitorial zeal left conference participants bruised and bloody. Recently, one beneficiary of this conference (as well as the "sunshine rounds" Seldin held at 6:00 a.m.) told me he bribed the chief resident with a bottle of scotch to put his chart on the bottom of the stack!

Four floors below, Dr. Robert McClelland, professor of surgery was showing surgical films to trainees in the operating room conference room, when he "heard a knock at the door." Reports differ as to who summoned McClelland. One recalls surgery professor Malcolm Perry entering the room, saying softly, "The president's been shot and they're bringing him here." McClelland recalls surgery resident Charles Crenshaw urgently beckoning him into the hall.

Many, like senior surgery resident Ron Jones, were having what passed as food in the Parkland cafeteria. Hearing the frantic staccato of emergency pages, he called the hospital operator and was told, "The president has been shot and they are bringing him to the emergency room and need physicians."

At Southwestern Medical School, only a hundred yards away, some of my sophomore classmates were waiting in our classroom for a pathology exam while others believed they were about to hear a lecture from Kemp Clark, who would never show up for it. Rick Cohen and I thought we remember sitting in the Parkland library when the frantic pages started, and we seem to recall Clark hurrying out after somebody ran up to him with the news. The freshmen were in the anatomy lab—some even managed to keep on with their dissections until mid-afternoon, listening to history unfold on the radio. Most of us, though, sprinted over to Parkland to join the death vigil outside the Parkland ER entrance. The CBS film of that moment shows our classmate Cervando Martinez hanging on to a "KEEP RIGHT" sign in the parking lot, as though the weight of that moment made it hard to stand unaided. He had seen the president at Love Field that morning, witnessed the blood drenched presidential limousine race by on the Stemmons Freeway, and now the dreadful finality of 1:00 p.m. when we learned our president was dead.

Courtesy of UT Southwestern Medical Center, Library Archives

The Parkland Hospital of the 1960s appears in this aerial shot. The oblong drive to the right leads to Southwestern Medical School, then only a few years old. The Cary and Hoblitzel buildings connect the medical school to Parkland. An underground tunnel ran under these buildings from the medical school to the hospital, and during the Cuban Missile Crisis a year before the assassination, emergency supplies were stored there. Southwestern was to become a world-class medical school, home to five Nobel Prize winners.

RON JONES, MD

(oral history courtesy of the Sixth Floor Museum)

I don't think that Parkland Hospital was as well-known prior to 1963 as it became known afterwards, although it was becoming recognized as a major teaching institution and particularly noted for its management of severely injured patients and the so-called "trauma" patient.

SAM DORFMAN, MD

The first we (the class) knew was the sirens as they emanated from town and then, even in the anatomy lab, we heard that the president had been shot and was en route to Parkland. While we were working on our cadavers, we kept an ear "glued" to the radio and eventually heard that he was dead. No one felt like working, so we left about three that afternoon.

GERALD HILL, MD

I was eating a ten cent lunch bag, which consisted of Fritos and a tuna sandwich, in the lecture room at noon. A classmate came in and told the four of us that Kennedy had been shot. He said the word was Secret Service shot the front up on a building. We hee-hawed at first, then went directly out the doors of the room to the grassy slope overlooking the ER entrance. . . . We saw some of the coming and going. He was already in the ER.

DONALD SELDIN, MD

Every Friday the Department of Medicine held a death conference in a large room which was located just one floor above the emergency room. In the middle of the conference one of our faculty members, Dr. Dan Foster, entered the room and interrupted the conference with the statement, "President Kennedy and Governor Connally have both been shot and are in our emergency room. I think the president is dying and Governor Connally is wounded in the arm." Dr. Foster looked pale and shaken; there was a stunned silence in the room.

Dr. Madison and I left the conference immediately and went down to the emergency room where there was chaos. Several Secret Service agents were moving about with machine guns in their hands. In the far end of the room was the president, who was attended by Dr. Kemp Clark, chief of neurosurgery and Dr. Pepper Jenkins, chief of anesthesiology. Dr. Jenkins was administering oxygen while Dr. Clark, Dr. McClelland, and Dr. Baxter were attending to the head wound.

I had heard a rumor to the effect that the president might have been suffering from adrenal insufficiency and wanted to make certain that he received large doses of hydrocortisone. It turned out that this had already been administered by Dr. Carrico, a surgical resident.

Dr. Jenkins was shaking his head muttering, "Last Rites." Mrs. Kennedy was sitting limply in a chair, her skirt spattered with blood and some buttery-looking material, presumably the president's brain tissue. Shortly after I arrived at the president's side, he was pronounced dead by Dr. Jenkins. I felt disarrayed and ineffectual and left the emergency room with a stunned feeling of incomprehension and agitation.

Daniel Foster, MD

On November 22, 1963, I was attending the weekly clinico-pathologic conference of the Department of Internal Medicine presided over by Dr. Donald W. Seldin, the chairman of the Internal Medicine Department. I was seated immediately in front of the door of the Doctors' Dining Room when I heard a knock on the door. I opened it and my close friend, Dr. John Brown, a rheumatologist, stood there. With no explanation he said the president had been shot and brought to Parkland Memorial Hospital. I came back into the dining room and Dr. Seldin said, "Dr. Foster, what is wrong?" (He later told me I was very pale.) The conference was canceled and Dr. Seldin headed to the emergency room. I was not involved in the remainder of the events.

I was a close friend of Dr. Jim Carrico, the chief resident of surgery. He was working in the surgery clinic and had been called to the emergency room to see two Parkland patients, one with a mechanical intestinal obstruction, the second with a thrombophlebitis with infection. He took another resident with him. There was no time to care for the Parkland patients because the mortally wounded president arrived. He was the first to see him and injected him with hydrocortisone, remembering that the president had adrenal insufficiency (Addison's disease).

When the presidential party left he returned to the patient with intestinal obstruction and operated on her.

We did not learn until a few days later that two other famous persons also died on November 22, 1963: the author/theologian, C. S. Lewis, and the author Aldous Leonard Huxley, whose best known novel was *Brave New World*.

BOB PERSILLIN, MD

As a fellow in rheumatology at the time, my recollections are clear. Certainly you will hear my story many times over in many different forms.

Ironically, it was the time of the Department of Medicine death conference at Parkland when JFK was brought to the ER. At that very excellent teaching conference, presided over by Dr. Seldin, patients who died in the hospital were presented and their care defended. Residents and even attending cowered at the scorn from His Holiness.

A junior assistant professor, Dr. John Baum, chronically late to the conference, was on his way when he was diverted by the commotion in the ER. When told what was transpiring, he rushed to the death conference glass door and hurriedly beckoned Dr. Seldin who ran to the ER, but quickly returned as the outcome was already clear.

H. Wayne Smith, MD

I was in my second year of internal medicine residency. Each Friday at noon we had a death conference with case presentations by house staff and discussion by one of the staff members. Dr. Don Seldin was talking when Dr. Dan Foster came in the room—white as a sheet—and announced that the president had been shot. The conference was immediately adjourned and Dr. Seldin immediately left.

Everyone was in shock. What I witnessed next was chaos in the halls of Parkland—TV commentators, media members, and miles of cables up and down the halls.

Rex Cole, MD

I was a third year medical student then. I was on the internal medicine rotation. We were in the chart room on the sixth floor and it was about noon. There was a conference in session and it was concluding. I was leaning against the wall and could see out the open windows toward the front of Parkland. I saw two black limousines speed by and proceed to the rear of the hospital. I remember thinking that was strange because I had never seen a limousine at Parkland before.

Shortly thereafter, I went down to the cafeteria to eat alone. As I was sitting there I heard the hospital operator page Dr. Tom Shires stat to the emergency room. Now that was truly out of the ordinary. Then I recall she paged stat to the emergency room in rapid succession Dr. Malcolm Perry, Dr. Kemp Clark (whom we naturally called "Man Super"), and I believe Dr. Charles Baxter. I thought something big must be happening. I noticed nothing out of the ordinary at that time.

Then I went back to the sixth floor. I saw the intern on our service, Ron Prati, in the hallway and he said, "Man! What a day!" I asked him what he meant and he said, "They shot Kennedy." I remember being confused, thinking that we didn't have a patient named Kennedy. Then he told me it was the president.

I recall an eerie silence on the floor the rest of the afternoon. There were no requests for PRN meds or other requests for service by the patients on the floor. Later I thought they were probably thinking about something other than themselves.

MICHAEL ELLSASSER, MD

In November 1963 Don Gilliard and I were third year ophthalmology residents, recently returning to Parkland from our V.A. rotation. On November 22, we were eating lunch in the cafeteria with Dr. John Lynn, who had been installed as the first full-time chief of ophthalmology in our absence. Getting better acquainted with one another, we had difficulty believing the rumor that quickly spread over the room that President Kennedy had been shot. In a few short minutes, however, we heard several sirens, and we ran to the windows overlooking the ER entrance. The presidential vehicles roared in, in apparent panic. I've never witnessed such pandemonium.

HARRY EASTMAN, MD

At the time President Kennedy was brought to Parkland, I was a senior medical student eating lunch on the floor above the emergency room with Charles Jenkins and Bill Scroggie. We heard the news and ran to the emergency room.

At that time Parkland ER had two trauma rooms—one was crowded with people and we could not see in the room, but were asked not to go in unless we were involved in the care of the president, so we did not. The other room appeared almost empty (we were not close), and Governor John Connally lay on a gurney with only perhaps one person attending to him. We didn't go in that room either.

BOB VAUGHAN, MD

My recollections of November 22, 1963, were punctuated by chaos and confusion as I remember that day. Our assembled class was receiving a lecture in the medical school auditorium by Dr. Kemp Clark, chief of neurosurgery, when he was interrupted abruptly by a stat page to the Parkland emergency room. Our class spilled out into the hallway to learn that *all* Clinical Chairs were paged stat to the PMH ER including the surgery chairman, Dr. Tom Shires. That never, ever happens . . . but it did!

RON JONES, MD

(oral history courtesy of the Sixth Floor Museum)

I would like to have seen the parade, but that morning I had surgery to perform and just couldn't get free. I came in that morning fairly routinely, and we had performed a vascular procedure—Dr. Perry and I had. And we had just completed that and had gone downstairs to the cafeteria when this event unfolded.

The reason that I answered the phone was that they were paging overhead, "Dr. Tom Shires, stat. Dr. Kemp Clark, stat." Dr. Shires was chief . . . chairman of the department of surgery. Dr. Kemp Clark was chairman of the division of neurosurgery. And several other physicians on the full-time attending staff were being paged stat. That was highly unusual. And as a matter of fact, I happen to know that Dr. Shires was out of town that day, and Dr. Perry and I were across the table from each other and began to look in some wondering astonishment as to why this was happening. And I said, "I'm going to go call the operator and see what's going on," and so, I actually called her. And she said, "Dr. Jones, the president's been shot, and they're bringing him to the emergency room." To my knowledge, that was the first indication that the staff at Parkland knew that anything had happened, and I presume that she had been called by the police or Secret Service to notify that they were en route to the hospital.

I hung up the phone and turned around and noticed a table. This was a fairly large cafeteria. And just a few feet away behind me sat Dr. M. T. Jenkins, who . . . [was] better known as "Pepper" Jenkins, and he was head of the department of anesthesia, and Miss Audrey Bell, who was the operating room supervisor at

Parkland. And so, people were beginning to look at me at that time from . . . employees in the cafeteria, knowing that something must be going on. I went over to that table, and I said, "You aren't going to believe this, but the president's been shot and they're bringing him to the emergency room." And Dr. Jenkins said, "Well, I'll get an anesthesia machine from the operating room and bring it right down." And Miss Bell said, "I'll get an operating room ready."

Another person at that table, I think, was Dr. George Beck, who was another anesthesiologist. And about that time, coming up the hall or the aisle in the cafeteria was Dr. Perry, with whom I had been eating, and Dr. James "Red" Duke, who was one of the junior residents at that time. And both of them asked me what was going on, and I said, "Well, let's go on out the back-door, but the president's been shot. And they want some people in the emergency room." And so, we went out the back of the cafeteria and down some back steps because we were on the . . . just one floor . . . we were on the ground floor or the first floor, and the emergency room was on the ground floor. So, we went down one floor, and we entered directly into the front part of the emergency room.

RON JONES, MD

(from *Baylor Reflections*)

On November 22nd, 1963, as a young chief surgery resident at Parkland Hospital having lunch in the cafeteria with Dr. Malcolm Perry, I suddenly heard several pages for various department chairmen over the loud speakers. This was before the age of beepers, and messages were obtained by prominently displayed lighted signs or the overhead speaker pages. I went to a telephone in the cafeteria, called the operator and asked why she was paging so many chairmen stat. She replied, "The president has been shot and they're bringing him to the emergency room and need physicians."

I experienced a tremendous rush of adrenaline and a flushed feeling throughout my body. As I turned around, I immediately saw the chairman of the Department of Anesthesiology and the operating room nurse supervisor and informed them. Dr. Marion Jenkins said, "I will go up to the operating room and bring down an anesthesia machine," and Ms. Bell said she would get the operating room ready. At that point I assumed that the president had been shot in a crowd and would undergo emergency surgery.

GEORGE MEKKER, MD

In 1963 I started a general surgery residency with several other Ohio State classmates, namely Irwin Thal, MD, Harlan Pollock, MD, and William Rae, MD

On November 22, 1963 I was on an anesthesiology rotation. At about midday I joined a group watching surgical movies monitored by Dr. Robert McClelland, professor of surgery I was late so I sat next to Dr. McClelland by the projector. Suddenly, Dr. Malcolm Perry, professor of surgery, entered the room, and softly, I overheard him say to McClelland, "The president's been shot and they're bringing him here." They exited and I followed.

ROBERT MCCLELLAND, MD

(oral history courtesy of the Sixth Floor Museum)

And there were a lot of interesting coincidences about my relationship with this Kennedy assassination.

It almost makes you think about—what is it?—the union synchronicity about how things seem to be associated, only they're not really associated and (these are) odd coincidences. And the first of them was in 1961. I think it was the fall when Rayburn [at the time the Speaker of the US House of Representatives] was here. My wife was taking care of him over at Baylor. She was working at Baylor at that time, and she was amused because they were always quoting what Sam had said in the paper. Sam was comatose virtually all the time that he was there [chuckling]. He never said anything to anybody, and yet he was apparently quoted fairly liberally on the TV and in the press and whatnot.

Because one day my wife said, "You know, I forgot to pick up my check at Baylor." And so, I was getting off early at Parkland that day. She said, "Would you drive over and pick it up?" And as I said, we were living over on Lipscomb, just off of Gaston at that time. So, I said, "Yeah, I'll pick it up on the way home."

And so I drove by over there, and I drove into the old Gaston Hospital parking lot and parked my little beat-up Volkswagen, and got out and was walking across the street . . . it must have been about three or four in the afternoon, something like that. And I was walking toward the side door of Baylor, which at that time had a side door, and there was a street there which is no longer there. And I noticed a bunch of children running out of that school that was next door to it. It was a . . . I think now it's some kind of medical magnate school, but then it was a grade school. So, it looked like a bunch of third or fourth graders were all excited and were running down the street toward Baylor. I thought, "Huh," you know, "what's that?" And then about that same time, around the corner there on Washington . . . was it Washington or ? . . . anyway, the street that comes right down toward Baylor, they turned onto Gaston about three or four Cadillac limousines and a bunch of motorcycle cops and whatnot, and I thought, "Well, that's interesting. I wonder who that is?" And this, you know, cortege of cars pulled up and pulled up to the side door and the lead limousine parked and by this time, I was probably less than the distance from here to . . . in fact, about half the distance from that thing (indicating something off-camera) and here to the rear door, which was opened by one of the motorcycle cops, and who should step out but John Kennedy. And I thought, "Well, how 'bout that, you know." [chuckling] "And I literally could have kind of leaned over and leaned out and touched him. Of course, they'd have shot me if I did that, but . . . [laughing] And I didn't do that, but I thought about that later. Now, what were the odds of me being what . . . doing what I was doing two years later and having been one out of several million people who could have been there to see him. Only, you know . . . there was no connection, but there was a connection, and the synchronicity sort of thing.

And another odd coincidence, just while I'm on that subject, is that the day he was assassinated, my wife had our two children at the time at the pediatrician's which was over in the Turtle Creek area of Dallas, so it was right by where they were coming by. So, the lady in the doctor's office . . . the receptionist told them, "Oh, the president's coming by here." So everybody went outside, and Connie was standing there holding our two children, and she almost could have leaned out and touched them. So, my wife saw them when they came back, and then thirty minutes later, I was helping take care of him.

And then two years after that, one of my friends who's . . . was it two or three years after? . . . anyway, some time after that, one of my friends said, "I've had a problem with a patient of mine that I did a gastrectomy on, and I wonder if I could get you to come over and see him for me. And I think we're going to have to operate on him because he's got some kind of complication." And I said, "Well, sure." It was over at Presbyterian. The patient was Mr. Zapruder." [smiling] [Zapruder is famous to this day because of his footage of the assassination itself.]

I was in a little conference room in the operating room, and I was showing a movie. I even remember what movie it was, about how to repair a hiatal hernia, to some of the residents. So, we had the movie projector going, and I heard this little knock on the door. And I went over to it and kind of opened the door, you know, and so Chuck was there. He was a resident at that time, and he said, "Come out here. I need to tell you something real important." And so, he told me. He said, "They're bringing the president in. He's been shot, and they want everybody to come downstairs." I said, "Well, OK." You know, so, I stuck my head back in the door and told one of the other residents, you know, to go on with showing the movie. I'd be back up, probably, shortly. And so, there was an elevator that went right down into the emergency room at that time, and so Dr. Crenshaw and I rode down into that, and we got off into the main part of the emergency room then, walked around the corner, and in the meantime, as we were coming down, I was telling Chuck, I said, "Well, you know, Chuck, this is probably nothing. We're always getting these rumors, you know, like some plane just crashed out at Love Field, and it turns out that somebody tripped and . . . you know, [chuckling] and it's magnified out of all proportion. And that's probably. . . ." "Oh, I don't know," he said. So, we continued on around into the main area of the pit, as we called it, and saw this huge crowd of people there, and as we went on back towards the back . . . I thought, Well, something's going on here. And then the crowd parted enough that I saw Mrs. Kennedy sitting there on a chair in that famous pink suit, and I thought, "Oh my God."

CHAPTER 4

"THE PIT"

In 1963, the emergency room at Parkland Hospital treated an average of 272 emergency cases a day. Every student practiced his or her skills there—stitching up trauma victims, delivering precipitously born babies, setting fractures, and diagnosing bipolar disorders. Saturday nights were especially peppered by gunshot wounds, giving students the impression that war was endemic in the streets of Dallas.

The emergency entrance was at the back of hospital, where an ambulance ramp led to double swinging doors opening into a thirty-foot corridor. This passage emptied directly into "The Pit," the draconian name for the Parkland ER.

The ER's surgery section had eight booths for examination and treatment, and four emergency operating rooms. Two of these, Trauma Room 1 and Trauma Room 2, were especially equipped for the most seriously injured. Many students, residents, and interns were in the hallways leading to Trauma Room 1, and in this chapter, they recall how they came to be so close to the unfolding tragedy, what they saw, and how they felt.

RON JONES, MD

(oral history courtesy of the Sixth Floor Museum)

We would usually see about, as I recall, about a thousand gunshot wounds and a thousand stab wounds a year and about five thousand automobile accident victims a year in the emergency room. The emergency room at Parkland was very busy. Well over 100,000 to 125,000 visits a year at that time. All of us had seen well over 100 or 200 gunshot wounds by the time we had completed a residency, and so that was not something that was new to us or was particularly disturbing to us.

LESLIE MOORE, MD

If the answer was accurate, I knew they would be taking him [the president] to Parkland, so my wife and I got up from our table immediately and headed out an exit door. No one else was visible in the parking lot; all seemed to have remained inside the building. We jumped in my VW beetle and headed over to Parkland. There was little traffic congestion as of yet and we pulled up to a side door to the Parkland library area. Already, there was a policeman guarding the door and he said I was not allowed in. I told him I was a doctor and had to get in and he acquiesced. I went down to the ER and a crowd was gathering, doctors, nurses, orderlies, Secret Service, and others. After a number of minutes, one of our professors, Fouad Bashour, MD, emerged from the trauma room (which was no more than fifteen feet away just around the corner) shaking his head and saying, "He's dead." Just those two words and that was it.

I went out of the ER to the emergency entrance and there was the limousine splattered with blood and there was a considerable amount of the president's blood on the sidewalk. Jackie Kennedy had been in the ER with her pink suit showing quite a bit of blood. I never saw her again.

Rumors began circulating in and around the ER that Vice President Lyndon Johnson, who had a history of more than one heart attack, was heading back to the emergency room with severe chest pains. Everyone was ready for whatever might come of this but apparently, it turned out to be just hearsay.

Robert Duchouquette, MD

I immediately made a u-turn and followed the limo to Parkland's ER. I entered the emergency entrance shortly after he was transferred to the largest ER trauma treatment room. In the confusion of others in scrubs, albeit mine were OB greens, I was witness to the frenzied resuscitative efforts displayed by the chiefs of all trauma-related services who had been called to the scene. As soon as he was placed from the gurney onto the emergency table, it was obvious from his ghastly head wound that he was DOA, and regardless of all the impressive medical acumen and experience present, there was no hope of restoring his life. He was flat-lined from the onset. However, the official word went out that physicians were working toward that end, and it was erroneously reported by the press that he was alive for thirty-five minutes after his fatal wound.

This delay in the announcement of his death was obviously used to secret Lyndon B. Johnson away on Air Force One, now vaulted into the presidency by this terrible act. Several minutes later, a Secret Service agent asked what my function was in the resuscitative efforts, and I had to admit it was "observation." Thus ended my visit with the president.

RONALD O. WYATT, MD

The first memory of that day, I was on my internal medicine rotation at Parkland Hospital. That morning was the day Dr. Selden questioned the medical students. A trying event! It was later in the morning when someone looked out the window as President Kennedy's entourage was passing by Parkland Hospital from Love Field on Harry Hines Boulevard. He was going downtown for a parade; I remember everyone in the class watching.

After being dismissed from class I took the elevator to the first floor to go to the cafeteria for lunch. Walking down the hall a nurse came by me and was crying. I stopped her and asked why she was crying. She said, "The president has been shot and is in the emergency room!" I couldn't believe it. I thus took some back steps to the ER. When I got there the door was blocked by the police and not allowing anyone in.

I then went to x-ray which had a door leading to the ER. I just stood there and watched in disbelief. As I looked, Mrs. Kennedy was brought into ER by the Secret Service. She was covered with blood. I then left. I remember the press, TV, etc. was at the hospital almost immediately with TV cameras, newspeople, cables running down hallways, etc. Med school was dismissed and I went home depressed.

JOHN HEARD, MD

I was in the cafeteria when over the PA system came the call for the heads of departments by name asap to the ER. Very strange. I went out of the cafeteria down the back stairs and opened the door to the ER hallway. A man with a gun spun toward me, looked me over carefully, and continued down the hall. Right behind him was Kennedy on a stretcher followed by Jackie in her pink, blood stained suit. Her face is what I remember most. I closed the door in shock and, being a good SW med student, went to take my pathology exam. They told us all to go home.

Abram "Chic" Eisenstein, MD

Two or three of our (freshman) class were stopped at the corner of Inwood and Lemon (trying to get to Kip's for lunch) by a motorcade which we then found out was Kennedy's. I am not sure we even knew he was coming to town—hey, we were sweating Gross Anatomy! After eating our burgers we went back to the school and as I was parking, someone yelled Kennedy had been shot and was coming to Parkland. We ran from the parking lot to the ER and got in before he arrived and the place was closed down. We hid in the hallway just watching. The stretcher came in with Jackie and then into surgery ER. Connally and LBJ followed.

Finally, we were told to leave and walked out into the driveway in front of the ER. I stayed there for what seemed like hours. The eerie thing was someone had a radio broadcasting from the national station's hook up. We knew how things really were thirty minutes before they were broadcast publicly. We saw the priest come in. We watched a poor Latino couple (she was pregnant) pull up to go to delivery. The SS guys grabbed the car and moments later four or five agents covering LBJ ran out of the ER and took the car to Love Field. I kept saying to myself that this was *real*, yet unbelievable! No cell phone to take pictures! I grabbed a small branch from a tree over me and kept it for years.

LARRY DOSSEY, MD

I was a first-year medical student at UT Southwestern in November 1963. A couple of my classmates and I had driven to a nearby eatery for lunch, and on returning to the medical school heard on the car radio that President Kennedy had been shot and had been rushed to Parkland Hospital.

Eager to know what was happening, I dashed into Parkland via the emergency room entrance amid unbelievable chaos. The ER entry area was packed and the din was indescribable, with people pushing and shouting at top volume. Suddenly a gentleman in coat and tie grabbed me by my arm. He introduced himself as Robert Pierpoint, the *CBS News* correspondent who was traveling with the presidential party. I recognized Pierpoint; he was nationally known, frequently appearing on CBS television evening news. He said to me with unmistakable urgency, "Can you help me?" Pierpoint had managed to capture one of the few pay telephones in the Parkland ER, and he was hanging onto it for dear life. On the other end of the line was the CBS office in New York City. "Will you guard this phone while I find out what's going on with the president?" he implored. I said yes. Then Pierpoint pushed his way down the hall to Trauma Room 1. While he was doing so, I was asked by the CBS people in New York what I could observe from my vantage point. I described the chaos as best I could. Then Pierpoint returned, took the phone, and provided the information he'd obtained in Trauma Room 1. He and I kept the telephone trading going for an hour or so.

Finally Pierpoint told the CBS office that the president was dead. I was unable to comprehend it. Pierpoint was obviously stricken with grief and disbelief. He simply said to me tearfully,

"Thank you for your help." For a moment we just stood there looking at each other, realizing we were participants in a drama we could not grasp, but which we would remember for the rest of our lives. Then he gathered himself and dashed off to pursue events unfolding outside in the ER parking lot that would involve Jacqueline Kennedy, Vice President Lyndon B. Johnson, and Judge Sarah T. Hughes.

STEPHEN BARNETT, MD

I have some very distinct recollections on that grim day fifty years ago.

Cervando and I were on top of Parkland checking out the new psych floor that was being added just before lunch. Suddenly cars flying and sirens yelling came over the hill at the juvenile detention center on Harry Hines Blvd. And I thought, "My god, they've killed the president." The night before, I'd been doing some research in the med school library. An 8 x 11 poster was circulated that night. It was a mug shot of JFK and below it said, WANTED, DEAD OR ALIVE FOR TREASON.

We ran for the elevator, but then I ran down the stairs for the ER. I arrived just as the president was slipped into the trauma room and Mrs. Kennedy was being led away. At that point, the Secret Service ushered me out of the ER entrance. About a half hour later, Vice President Johnson was shuffled out and into the back seat of an old model car and whisked away.

I remember feeling stunned, at a loss to respond, confused between sorrow and rage, but left in an empty hole the rest of the afternoon.

And that's the way it was, for this observer.

JAMES CARRICO, MD

(oral history courtesy of the Sixth Floor Museum)

I don't remember the early morning. Actually, I was assigned to Surgery C, which is an elective surgery service, and it was our day to admit patients. So, we came in . . . I'm confident we came in early that morning and made rounds. It was also our clinic day. We didn't operate that day. We had our . . . basically, our office. So, we . . . early in the morning, probably 8:30 or 9:00, went over to our clinic to start seeing patients, both patients we had operated on and patients who were being evaluated for new operations.

About 11:30, we were getting pretty close to getting through with our clinic, and we got a call from the emergency room saying that there were three patients down there to be evaluated for admission. This was not President Kennedy. This would be for three patients who had come to Parkland for care. And one of our service needed to go down there and start seeing those patients and evaluating them. We also had scheduled a special x-ray where a patient, you know, had blood clots in his lungs, and somebody had to go down and participate in doing that x-ray study. The x-ray study sounded like a lot more fun than working up three patients, so Jerry Gustafson, who was a year ahead of me in the program, and I flipped. And he won the coin flip. He had the privilege of going to do the X-ray study, and I went down to the emergency room to start evaluating the patients that we were going to end up admitting. So, that's how I got down in the emergency room.

Dallas really did have a sophisticated system for the time, but it consisted of some of the ambulances having radios which connect with the police dispatcher and the police dispatcher would then call the hospital and say, you know, "x" patients are coming. There was frequently some confusion in all that communication with several people. So, a lot of times, we got a call from a police dispatcher which turned out to be a false alarm or overstated. So, that leads up to what happened then. We . . . one of the nurses came out and told Dick Delaney, Richard Delaney, who was actually in charge of the emergency room that day, that she just got a call from the police dispatcher, and the president had been shot and was on his way to the hospital.

That's all. That's the message I remember. The president's been shot and is on his way to the hospital. [smiling] The obvious question is: what do you do? Well, the first thing you do is . . . you don't want to believe it. You know, and with all the misinformation that happened in a situation like that, it was easy to say, "Nah. It must be wrong. I mean, it can't be right." But the other thing you do is . . . you start to get ready. So, we had the nurses page the appropriate people to come help take care of an injured patient. They paged the chief surgery team, the emergency team, the rest of the emergency team on call, the chief resident who was Ron Jones, who is now the Chief of Surgery at Baylor Hospital.

We hoped very much that it was a false alarm. [laughing] Right? Of course, there's always the risk that you would get called in on a false alarm. Anyway, it seemed like two or three minutes after we got the message that the door to the emergency room came open and a patient was rolled in. And that was Governor Connally, as a matter of fact, and the reason Governor Connally was brought in first is because he was sitting in the jump seat. Right, so they had to get the governor out of the way, and they brought him in first. So, we looked at Governor Connally, and he had a large wound in the front of his chest and was actually unconscious from the abnormal breathing that results from that large wound. We knew he was hurt badly. We figured we could treat him, if that was all that was wrong. And we also knew that that wasn't the president. It didn't occur to either Delaney or I who it was. We were only interested in who it wasn't. And it was not the president, so we kind of heaved this great sigh of relief and said, "Maybe it's a Secret Service man, but we'll take care of him." So, we wheeled him into Trauma Room 2, which is really the biggest trauma room.

But basically, Delaney and I both went in the room with him. We knew the rest of the support was on the way. The way you treat a wound like that is you plug the hole. Basically, when you breathe, air normally goes in here. If you got a hole this big [holding area under his right armpit], air goes in there. So, you plug that hole. Then, the air starts going in the right way, and the governor started waking up. So, about that time, another patient was rolled into Trauma Room 1, and Delaney and I kind of looked at each other and I'm not sure how we decided, but basically, we decided that Delaney would stay with the governor and I'd go see the patient in the other room. And that's how I ended up being in the president's room.

Robert McClelland, MD

(excerpted from *D Magazine*, November 2008)

He begins the narrative he's told so many times. "I heard a knock at the door." McClelland says. At the door was Dr. Charles Crenshaw. He asked McClelland to step into the hall for a moment. When he returned, McClelland turned off the projector and left the students. The two doctors moved immediately to the elevator.

In the elevator, McClelland tried to reassure Crenshaw. He mentioned that there had been a lot of alarming stories from the emergency room recently, and most cases turned out not to be too bad.

When the elevator doors opened, they turned right and saw a wall of dark suits and hats. ("Everyone wore hats in those days," he tells the students. Their conceptions of that time come mostly from a film made in 1991.)

The open area at the center of the emergency room was called "the pit." Neither doctor had ever seen the pit so jammed with people: Secret Service men, nurses, medical students, residents, reporters, photographers, and curious bystanders.

In the shuffle, the dark suits parted. About 50 feet away, McClelland could see Jackie Kennedy seated outside Trauma Room One. Her pink dress was covered in blood.

"This is really what they said it was," he said quietly to Crenshaw.

McClelland thought for a moment that he might be the most senior faculty member on site. His boss, Dr. Tom Shires, chair of the department of surgery, was in Galveston at a meeting of the Western Surgical Association. Because it was near lunch, he worried the other doctors might be off the premises. ("The food was so bad at the hospital," he tells the students, "we often went out to the hamburger place across the street.")

His instincts were to move the other direction, but he forced himself to keep walking toward Trauma Room One, fighting through the crowd. A large woman named Doris Nelson stood in front of the doors, directing traffic, her voice bellowing above the bedlam. She was the nurse director of the emergency room. She told the Secret Service men who was allowed in and whom to keep out. When McClelland and Crenshaw arrived, she waved them in.

CHAPTER 5

GOVERNOR CONNALLY

Texas Governor John Connally was seated in front of JFK when the assassin's bullet ripped through the president and pierced the Governor's chest, shattering his wrist on exit. The sucking chest wound could have proven fatal in the first few minutes after arrival at the Parkland ER, as all the attention was on the president in Trauma Room 1.

Senior med student Bill Scroggie came upon Connally momentarily unattended and, noting his respiratory distress, quickly found James "Red" Duke, the senior resident in chest surgery. Duke told Scroggie to find a nurse and some chest tubes, which Duke promptly inserted. This relieved the pneumothorax, which had collapsed his lung, and saved the Governor's life. Connally's letter of gratitude to the Parkland staff is reproduced from the *Parkland Papers*, November 30, 1963.

Governor Connally was to return to Parkland and Southwestern in the spring, when he addressed the graduating class of 1964. Leslie Moore remembers, "We all commented, amongst ourselves, how strong his grip was in shaking our hands in spite of having had a splintered radius from the attack."

PARKLAND BECOMES SEAT OF GOVERNMENT

As Governor John Connally, lay recuperating from the wounds inflicted by the assassins bullets, many changes took place in the routine of Parkland Memorial Hospital.

Governor Connally continued to run the business of the State of Texas from his hospital bed. Bill Stinson, administrative assistant to the Governor, set up a special office in a portion of the administrative suite and the Texas Department of Public Safety established a radio communication center in the Nursing Service Office.

In addition to Mr. Stinson, Maurine Ray, personal secretary to the Governor, and Joan Kennedy, secretary to Mr. Stinson who staffed the office full time, many other aides and volunteers worked out of the office.

George Christian, administrative assistant for news and public relations and Julian Read, press aide, were on hand for about the first week.

Howard Rose, executive assistant and Larry Temple, administrative assistant to the Governor, visited briefly from Austin.

Judge Merrill Connally, the Governor's brother represented the family and received the many guests and well wishers.

State Highway Patrolmen, who are responsible for the Governor's safety, were assisted by the Dallas Police Department and hospital security guards in establishing proper security measures at Parkland. The Highway Patrolmen were under the command of Col. Homer Garrison, Jr., Director of Texas Department of Public Safety, and Major Guy Smith, regional commander, Dallas Region.

MAYBE YOU HAVEN'T REALIZED – – – – –

* It was in the Parkland Memorial Hospital Emergency Room where Vice President Lyndon B. Johnson became the President of the United States at the moment of death of the late President Kennedy.
* At the time the dying President and wounded Governor were brought into the Emergency Room, there were 23 other patients undergoing treatment in the area. Seven additional emergency patients were admitted and treated between the time of arrival of the President and Governor at 12:38 p.m. and the removal of the President's body at 2:19 p.m.
* Every employee of the Dallas County Hospital District, whether working with the President, the Governor, another patient or performing regular duties contributed to the successful handling of the situation.
* Members of the press from around the nation and throughout the world have visited Parkland Memorial Hospital and telephoned in for information on the manner in which this emergency was managed.

EXCERPTS FROM A FEW OF THE MANY COMMUNICATIONS RECEIVED

Our hearts have been with you and your team in these tragic days. You have carried on in the finest tradition under what must have been the most trying circumstances. Your ef-

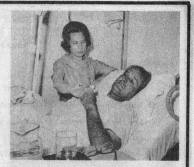

Governor and Mrs. John Connally shown in the Governor's hospital room immediately following his first press conference which was televised nationally Wednesday, November 27.

forts will stand as an example for all hospitals.

Stewart Hamilton, M.D.
Immediate Past President
American Hospital Association

On behalf of the KXOL reporters who covered the tragic assassination of President Kennedy and the wounding of Governor Connally, I wish to express my sincere thanks to your hospital staff. Our reporters at the scene told me they received every possible cooperation from your staff members in such a trying situation.

Roy Eaton
News Director, KXOL
Fort Worth, Texas

At a special meeting held on Monday, November 25, 1963, the Hospital Council Board of Directors asked me to extend the heartfelt congratulations of the 182 members of this Council to Parkland Memorial Hospital for the outstanding manner in which the hospital and its personnel conducted themselves during the recent tragedies surrounding the death of President Kennedy.

Your deportment at a time of extreme emergency held up for the entire nation an image of hospitals at their finest.

Henry X. Jackson
President
Hospital Council of Southern California

Every Auxiliary member I have talked with this past awful week has echoed the same sentiment, "How proud we are of Parkland, the way its staff rose so magnificently to the occasion, and how providential it was that the Emergency Room was so expertly redesigned and reorganized to serve so well in this and other emergencies."

When the eyes of all the world were on Dallas, this most important service of all was exactly right. We can all be so thankful for the fine leadership in our hospital, and in our great country that will enable us all to carry on in the best American tradition.

Mrs. Philip Van Horn Gerdine
President
The Women's Auxiliary to the
Dallas County Hospital District

The Medical Advisory Council unanimously voted to commend the Hospital Administrative Officers, the Medical Staff, the Hospital Employees, the Volunteers, and the Women's Hospital Auxiliary for the prompt and effective way in which they dealt with the medical emergencies produced by the assassination of the President of the United States and the other tragic events of the past several days.

In no small measure the Hospital Staff's ability to function so well was made possible by the recent expansion of physical facilities and increase in personnel in the Emergency Area. The Medical Advisory Council expresses its gratitude to the Hospital Board for these improvements.

Harry M. Spence, M.D.
Chairman, Medical Advisory Council
Dallas County Hospital District

Bill Stinson, center, administrative assistant to Governor John Connally, and chief of the temporary office established at Parkland Memorial Hospital, is shown with Col. Homer Garrison, Jr., left, Director of Texas Department of Public Safety and Highway Patrolman H. D. Jacks, who was driver for President Lyndon B. Johnson at the time of the assassination.

James "Red" Duke, MD

I was a senior resident, on the thoracic surgery service in November 1963. After being informed of the circumstances, I went immediately to the ER As I entered Trauma Room 1 and put on a pair of gloves, I noticed three faculty members dealing with the wound in the president's throat. As I walked around the head of the table, I saw the devastating wound in his head. I do not remember what I said, but I was told that there was a man across the hall that needed some help. I did not know who he was until later, but he did have a life threatening chest wound. I initiated the measures necessary to stabilize him and prepare him for surgery. I spent the next forty-eight hours with him.

James Carrico, MD

(oral history courtesy of the Sixth Floor Museum)

After I left Governor Connally's room, his treatment was rapidly taken over by the thoracic surgery service, by Dr. Robert Shaw and the resident on his team. They took Governor Connally up and operated on him. Dr. Shires, who had been in Galveston, was notified what was going on, and the story is that he was back in Texas . . . back in Dallas, excuse me, within about thirty minutes. Went on a helicopter from Galveston to Houston, and a military jet from Houston to Dallas. So, he was actually involved in checking the wound in Governor Connally's leg. But then he was in the hospital, I think, for about a week to ten days. The major problem was getting his chest wall closed and giving his lung a chance to get well. So, I really was not involved in his care but was aware of what was going on.

Norman Borge, MD

Governor Connally was unattended for several minutes, gasping for breath with a collapsed lung, until a resident inadvertently walked into the room and saw what was going on.

WILLIAM SCROGGIE, MD

I was in scrubs and told the Secret Service agent who I was and he let me go in. I ran to the hallway that led to the Trauma Room, and there was such a crowd I couldn't get near the place. I went back toward where I came in and there was this large area sectioned off with drapes and containing gurneys. There was a man on one of them completely unattended. I went over to take a look and recognized him right away. It was Governor Connally with a sucking chest wound. About that time, "Red" Duke comes around the corner, and I yelled at him to come quick: he did. He told me to get a nurse and chest tubes. I did and he put the chest tubes in while I watched and helped a little. I am sure this saved the Governor's life. He was in severe distress and cyanotic [his skin had a bluish cast due to lack of oxygen] before the chest tubes. The Governor was very appreciative and gave the commencement address at our graduation.

WILLIAM ZEDLITZ, MD

I left her [Mrs. Kennedy] and went across the hall to where Governor John Connally was lying on a gurney. He had an IV in place and a chest tube had been inserted and was being treated by Dr. James "Red" Duke who was the surgery resident rotating through the Chest Surgery service at that time. I asked him how he was feeling and if I could get him some pain medication and he answered that he was uncomfortable but didn't need anything at the present. I then turned and went back to the emergency room proper to see if anyone else had been injured and could not find any other casualties.

LESLIE MOORE, MD

Governor John Connally was also severely wounded during the assassination of the president and he was attended to by thoracic surgeon, Robert Shaw, MD. Dr. Shaw was a friend of my family and he recounted that in his years in the Korean War as a frontline surgeon and in several years of thoracic surgery in Afghanistan he had never seen so severe a chest wound!

Governor Connally recovered and was at our medical school graduation to hand us our diplomas. We all commented, amongst ourselves, how strong his grip was in shaking our hands in spite of having had a splintered right radius from the attack.

GEORGE MEKKER, MD

Awhile later, in the anesthesia lounge, I was instructed to get anesthesia ready in Room 9, the neurosurgery operating room. After that, Governor John Connally was brought up to the hallway outside the thoracic operating room. I was instructed to stand by with him. At the time, he had chest tubes and a right forearm splint. The thoracic surgical team arrived shortly and I turned Governor John Connally over to Dr. William Taylor, MD, the senior thoracic surgery resident who made preparations with the team for Dr. Shaw, a thoracic surgery professor who shortly arrived. They did a thoracotomy and repaired his right lung. I was through after the transfer of the governor to the operating room.

MICHAEL ELLSASSER, MD

Texas Governor John Connally had been wounded during the attack and was in Parkland for a time. The hospital was pretty much locked down: one had to be identified by a staff member to get in.

LEWIS RANEY, MD

On Monday I went to the OR for my scheduled surgery. I was greeted by someone who identified me. I don't remember identification badges, but we had names on our white coats. I was told that Governor Connally was or had been in surgery. This occurred for several days.

WILLIAM MAYS OSBORNE, MD

I was in surgery when we heard on the radio that John F. Kennedy had been shot while riding in a motorcade. When I finished surgery I went to the resident's call room to lie down. Soon after I lay down the phone rang and the operator said that Dr. Charles F. Gregory, under whom I was training in orthopedic surgery, needed me in surgery. I went to surgery and the room where Governor John Connally was. Dr. Shaw was already operating on the governor's chest. Dr. Gregory told me we were to operate on Connally's right wrist. After scrub and drape of the operative field, we started debriding the edges of the wound. The bullet had pierced his cashmere black coat and carried in a lot of small hairs. The distal radius was fractured, but didn't need any internal fixation. The wound on the volar side of the wrist was debrided and sutured. The dorsal wound was left open for drainage, and closed several days later when there was no evidence of infection. Skin traction to the right thumb was applied with elastic bands which were secured to a halo which was then secured to a cast. The bullet fragment that pierced his wrist had traveled on and gone into his left thigh.

Connally had been riding in the jump seat in front of Kennedy, so a single bullet could have pierced Kennedy's head and glazed Connally's axilla and chest then traveled through his wrist and lodged in his thigh.

These are the facts as I remember them.

Ron Jones, MD

(oral history courtesy of the Sixth Floor Museum)

I didn't see him [Connally] at any time or had the opportunity to even see his wounds, but he had a serious injury. There's no question that he had a major defect in his left chest and major injury to his left lung, and I think Dr. Shaw did a magnificent job in getting him to the operating room and repairing that. The injury to the wrist was somewhat disabling but not life-threatening, and as I recall, he had no significant injury to the leg that was explored. So, his main injury was to the chest, and once that was handled, then I think everybody thought he—short of any unseen sudden death problem—was going to survive. There was concern, I think, for security [nodding], for his security, and as I recall, there were metal sheets put over the windows in two or three rooms so that he could be moved from one room to the other. And they were concerned that somebody might try to shoot him from the outside because at that point, over that weekend, most of us didn't know what had triggered all of this and whether this was much broader . . . and what was the cause . . . what was the reason for the assassination? Was this some type of overthrow of the government? I mean, everything was considered at that point, and when Oswald was shot, it really got everybody's attention because we were seeming to relive the whole thing again.

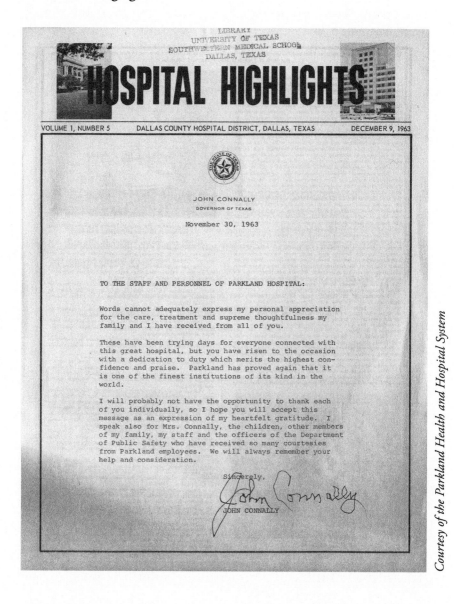

LIBRARY
UNIVERSITY OF TEXAS
SOUTHWESTERN MEDICAL SCHOOL
DALLAS, TEXAS

HOSPITAL HIGHLIGHTS

VOLUME 1, NUMBER 5   DALLAS COUNTY HOSPITAL DISTRICT, DALLAS, TEXAS   DECEMBER 9, 1963

JOHN CONNALLY
GOVERNOR OF TEXAS

November 30, 1963

TO THE STAFF AND PERSONNEL OF PARKLAND HOSPITAL:

Words cannot adequately express my personal appreciation for the care, treatment and supreme thoughtfulness my family and I have received from all of you.

These have been trying days for everyone connected with this great hospital, but you have risen to the occasion with a dedication to duty which merits the highest confidence and praise. Parkland has proved again that it is one of the finest institutions of its kind in the world.

I will probably not have the opportunity to thank each of you individually, so I hope you will accept this message as an expression of my heartfelt gratitude. I speak also for Mrs. Connally, the children, other members of my family, my staff and the officers of the Department of Public Safety who have received so many courtesies from Parkland employees. We will always remember your help and consideration.

Sincerely,

JOHN CONNALLY

Courtesy of the Parkland Health and Hospital System

CHAPTER 6

TRAUMA ROOM 1

As with much of history, a very big event occurred in a very small space.

Green tile covered the walls of Trauma Rooms 1 and 2, to a height of seven feet. This was necessary due to the tendency of many trauma victims to spurt blood all over the place like Jackson Pollock paintings. The twenty-by-twenty-foot Trauma Room 1 was one of four emergency operating theaters of the Parkland ER, and every medical student who graduated from Southwestern had some kind of hands-on experience in these trauma rooms. Two senior medical students had the most unforgettable experience of their lives that November day.

Joe D. Goldstrich had operated with Kemp Clark that morning, as he related in chapter four of Bill Sloan's *JFK: Breaking the Silence*, one of the plethora of conspiracy books. An early arrival in Trauma Room 1, he remained in the room until Kemp Clark pronounced the president dead. Goldstrich told me recently that he still believes the neck wound was a nickel-sized *entry wound*. Another senior in the room was Larry Klein, who observed the rescue effort from the feet of the dying president.

Staff anesthesiologists, Adolph "Buddy" Giesecke and Gene Aikin, attached the heart monitor, brought in by cardiac fellow, Riyad Taha, who also wheeled in the closet-sized pacemaker machine. No heartbeats were recorded.

Urology chairman, Paul Peters, arrived at the same time as Kemp Clark, and Clark began external cardiac massage. Moments later Peters inserted the right chest tube. Senior surgery resident Ron Jones arrived and, in less than a minute, achieved venous access by cutting down on the left cephalic vein. He then inserted the left chest tube.

Then Kemp Clark told them all to stop. *How* he told them requires its own chapter.

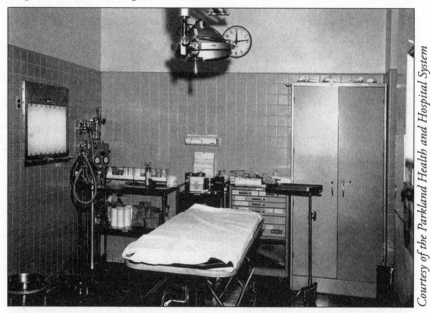

Courtesy of the Parkland Health and Hospital System

It is difficult to imagine how much of history was compressed into such a small space as Trauma Room 1. All the equipment used in the resuscitation effort was purchased by the National Archives at the request of the Kennedy family. Lenexa, Kansas, is home to the 300 square-foot, underground space—about the size of Trauma Room 1—where the artifacts are permanently secured.

JAMES CARRICO, MD

(excerpted from *The Texas State Journal of Medicine*, January 1964)

Editor's note: This is how *The Texas State Journal of Medicine* reported the actions and observations of second year surgery resident, Jim Carrico, MD Dr. Carrico's more personal reflections were recorded on videotape by the Sixth Floor Museum. Highlights of that fascinating interview appear below, courtesy of the Sixth Floor Museum.

> *Dr. Carrico was the first physician to see the president. A 1961 graduate of Southwestern Medical School, he is 28 and a resident in surgery at Parkland.*
>
> *He reported that when the patient entered the emergency room on an ambulance carriage he had slow agonal respiratory efforts and occasional cardiac beats detectable by auscultation. Two external wounds were noted; one a small wound of the anterior neck in the lower one third. The other wound had caused avulsion of the occipitoparietal calvarium and shredded brain tissue was present with profuse oozing. No pulse or blood pressure were present. Pupils were bilaterally dilated and fixed. A cuffed endotracheal tube was inserted through the laryngoscope. A ragged wound of the trachea was seen immediately below the larynx. The tube was advanced past the laceration and the cuff inflated. Respiration was instituted using a respirator assistor on automatic cycling. Concurrently, an intravenous infusion of lactated Ringer's solution was begun via catheter placed in the right leg. Blood was*

drawn for typing and cross-matching. Type 0 Rh nega-
tive blood was obtained immediately.

In view of the tracheal injury and diminished breath
sounds in the right chest, tracheostomy was performed by
Dr. Malcolm O. Perry and bilateral chest tubes inserted.
A second intravenous infusion was begun in the left arm.
In addition, Dr. M. T. Jenkins began respiration with
the anesthesia machine, cardiac monitor and stimu-
lator attached. Solu-Cortef (300 mg.) was given intra-
venously. Despite those measures, blood pressure never
returned. Only brief electrocardiographic evidence of
cardiac activity was obtained.

ALLEN CHILDS, MD

I remember Jim when I was a junior med student and he, then in
his third year of surgical training, was my resident. Years later I
was gratified he remembered me, and we had a laugh about how
we smoked in the halls between patient rooms. During rounds,
a Phillip Morris was always lit in an ashtray on the rolling chart
rack.

But what was most compelling about this bigger-than-
life person was his kindness toward the patients. He would
apologize for a painful procedure and I once heard him tell a
diagnostically obscure patient, "I still don't know what's wrong
with you." His humility was as evident as his deeply felt caring,
and it imprinted upon students like me an ideal we could try
to emulate.

JAMES CARRICO, MD

(oral history courtesy of the Sixth Floor Museum)

Mrs. Kennedy was kind of standing by the door. My recollection is that there were two men in the room, and I assume they were the driver or Secret Service people. They very rapidly stepped aside when we came in.

There was a nurse, Diana Bowron, and two interns, including Marty White who is now head of the organ bank here in Dallas . . . there's a lot of people still around, and an oral surgery resident whose name I don't remember right now. Oral surgery intern . . . so that was the team. Your job is a patient who is extremely injured, it kind of goes in the steps . . . do what it takes to keep the patient alive, then you go back and evaluate the injuries in more detail, and kind of make a long-term plan. And to keep him alive, first you've got to have a way to breathe, second you've got to be breathing, third your heart's got to be pumping, and fourth your head has to be working, your nervous system has got to be working.

So, your job is exactly that. You see what's going on with the air ways, you see what's going on with the breathing, you see what's going on with the circulation. And then, you look at neurological function. Usually, one person kind of takes charge and everybody else . . . one team gets some . . . the IVs going to support circulation, the nurse kind of gets the patient undressed and keeps things flowing.

And that's pretty much what we did. Marty White and the other intern started doing a cutdown on the president's right ankle, I think. Cutdown is where you start an IV by actually making an incision and putting the tube . . . or a big tube in the vein so you can give a lot of blood fluid if you need to. Diane and I looked at the president overall, saw that he was not breathing . . . he (was) breathing very erratically. We call it agonal respiration . . . a kind of gasping.

We looked at him, and he still had some breathing and he still had some heartbeat. He had a terrible looking wound, but that wound you kind of really deferred to later in terms of evaluating in detail.

The principle is, if you've got somebody who's got what looks like a terrible injury and is not dead, the first thing you do is you do the things I talked about. You get the airway going, you get him breathing . . . then you see . . . then you have time to evaluate the extent of the injury. My . . . I've told folks before that the thoughts that I remembered going through my head takes longer to describe them than it took to have them. The first one I had was . . . the president's had it. I mean, he's not going to make it. And that was right. Second is, we've got to do something. That was the political and the medical thoughts. You know, we can't just let the president die. [smiling] Third thought was . . . gosh, what if we get him alive and then he's a vegetable? And the rational thought was treat this patient like anybody else. Get his airway under control, get him breathing, get his circulation going . . . then, you can decide about all that other situation. So, that's what we did.

Oh, those brief thoughts . . . and, you know, it took a long time to say them, it took about that long to have them [snapping fingers] . . . were the non-medical thoughts. I guess my major thoughts were . . . you know, I really didn't think about the historical impact, what this is going to do. I thought, "Our job is to take care of the president." And we've got kind of this reputation of medicine and everything else on our back for a second there, and then that's when the rational thoughts took over. And I said, "OK, we know how to do this, I mean, whether this is the president or whoever. We know how to take care of this guy." And so, it became pretty much unemotional and auto . . . not automatic, but dispassionate at that point.

So, there was that short personal emotional "what am I going to do?" feeling, and then the professional aspect, as you say, kicked in, and you know what to do. It's what you're trained to do. So, the procedure then is to first see if the president is breathing . . . see if he has an airway. And he really didn't. When we looked at him, he had . . . we saw this wound in the side of his head [holding right side of head], a great big wound.

The president was lying on his back . . . I could see the whole wound in his head. And that's important, because it really doesn't fit perfectly with what we wrote down later. So, that meant it had to be in the . . . well, it was about right here as I recall [placing hand on right side of head, toward the back], and it was about as big as I'm showing it with my hand [opening hand about grapefruit size]. You know, a big chunk of bone and scalp missing, and the fact that you could see all of it from the front meant that it involved the parietal bone which is this big skull bone and the temporal bone which is this big skull bone. So, we saw that hole. We saw he had a little hole. . . .

By the time I looked, Diane, the nurse, had started taking his clothes off . . . which was her job. So, I really don't know whether it was through the collar or not but it was certainly through the collar line. Just above right there [placing finger right at the edge of his collar line], just to the right of the trachea and just certainly where his collar should have been.

OK. Anyway, so the next thing, since he wasn't breathing very well, the next to do is to try to get him breathing better, and that involves putting in the tracheal tube, which is a tube that goes through the mouth down into the windpipe, and you can breathe through it. So, he got that done. And at that time, we could see that there was some blood beside the larynx, which is done deep in the throat. From the inside.

When I looked down there, I could see that there was some bruising and some abnormal swelling off over to the right side of the windpipe, and we were able to slip the tube into his trachea, and he should have been able to breathe better at that point.

The other is that that wound [holding his head], this wound certainly looked like an exit wound. I mean, just because things were really blown away. It looked like, I mean, you've got . . . wounds go in and wounds go out. This was an out, that's what it looked like. There was nothing about it that would say whether the entrance had come from the front or from the back. This looked like where a bullet went out [holding side of head].

See, you try to keep the patient alive, you try to treat their wounds, then in the patients where you are not successful, then we would work with the medical examiner to try to help them figure out the forensics. They do the . . . they were really the forensic experts. We provided the clinical information.

. . . the only wounds I saw . . . the only wounds we saw were this wound here [pointing to center of neck] and this big hole here [placing right hand on side of head]. We never saw the wounds in the president's back. And the medical process is, we get his airway going, then we hooked him up to the ventilator and were trying to help him breathe. Then, you've got to answer, "How's his breathing going?" And to answer that, you've got to ask, "Are there any major holes in his chest wall, like the governor had in his chest wall, which would impair his breathing?" So, you don't always roll the patient over to look at that, particularly in the situation we're in, you don't roll him over. You just put your hands around the patient's back, down about the belt and then you kind of move up, feeling to try to make sure the body cavities are intact. And in doing that, I did not detect any big holes and obviously did not see what turned out to be two small wounds . . . one kind of over his shoulder and one back here . . . way back in the lower back of the head. So, we never saw those two wounds in the back. And that's the long answer to a short question [smiling].

And the reason we didn't is that that was, at least at that point, not part of an appropriate medical exam to try to find . . . that would have actually required rolling the patient over, washing the blood off, etc. And clearly in somebody that you're struggling to keep alive, you can't do that. After we got the tube in, tried to breathe for him, he still wasn't breathing very well, and his heart rate was slowing down. And his heart actually stopped. When his heart stopped, by that time, Dr. Perry, Dr. Jones, Dr. Jenkins, Dr. Giesecke that assisted chief of anesthesia, Dr. Baxter . . . a number of people were there. They started CPR. Because there were concerns of whether he had [indecipherable medical term] and we hadn't had time to get an x-ray, they actually put chest tubes in both chests, those are things so that if you do have a collapsed lung, it can expand it, and you can breathe. Concern about whether or not the tracheal tube was where it should be because of the tracheal wounds. Dr. Perry did a tracheotomy, which is where you make an incision in the neck to get a shorter tube in more directly into the trachea so there's no question it's in place. And I guess all that is important in terms of explaining what was done, and a lot of things happened in those twenty minutes. As I'm sure you're aware, the tracheotomy wound was right through this wound [pointing to side of neck] . . . I'm sorry, this wound in the neck [moving finger to center of neck]. And that caused some confusion later, but that's where a tracheotomy had to be. Then, we gave him some steroids because we had remembered from some stuff in the press that he probably had abnormal adrenal glands.

At this point, we had gotten his airway under control, had gotten him breathing, trying to make his circulation better . . . his circulation wasn't getting better. It was getting worse. His heart had stopped, but we had done all we could to get things stable. Kemp Clark, who was the chief of neurosurgery, evaluated the situation, evaluated the head wound in much more detail than I did. Kemp Clark was the one [who] actually pronounced him dead. Dr. Clark said . . . he basically said, "It's time to stop the resuscitation." For whatever reason, the decision was made to not actually pronounce the president dead until after the priest had come in and given him the Last Rites. So, we stopped treatment, but Dr. Clark didn't pronounce him till after the Last Rites.

Well, from that point, my part . . . the medical part, I guess, the patient care part of my job was over . . . had two things to do. One thing we had to do, as we do for all patients, was write a brief report for the emergency room records of the treatment, what we saw and what we did. And my other job was to find those three patients who I had been working on before the president came in and take care of them. We did sit down [smiling]. Well, I remember one thing that's probably . . . walked out of the trauma room #1 at the end of the big emergency room which twenty minutes before had been a big city county emergency room full of people being treated, etcetera. All the patients were gone when I walked out. They had been moved elsewhere. The people in the room were by-and-large, men with coats off, shirts and ties on, and guns on their hips. And a couple were on the phone talking to Washington. That's when, I guess really, the whole thing hit me, you know? Up till then, except for that brief moment, it had been professional work. I walked out there and realized that not only had my little world changed . . . that the whole world had changed. It had changed that quick [snapping fingers]. So, I smoked at that time as a lot of us did. We thought it was a cute thing to do, right? So, I started to light a cigarette, and imagine lighting a cigarette in an emergency room now? [laughing] But that was common in 1963. So, I started to light a cigarette and realized I was trembling so that I really couldn't . . . had trouble getting the match to the cigarette. But kind of got that under control, and I sat down to write my recollections. . . .

William Zedlitz, MD

After the repair was finished on a patient I was attending and the patient was taken to the recovery room and post-op orders had been written, I was sitting in the surgery office talking to one of the other residents when a page came in on the overhead speaker asking for Dr. Shires to go to the emergency room stat. Since Dr. G. Tom Shires was chief of surgery and chairman of the department of surgery, no one pages him to go anywhere, and since I knew Dr. Shires was not in town at that time, I decided to go down to the ER to see what the urgency was.

As I stepped off the elevator into the ER, a well-dressed man wearing a suit and tie and holding a rapid-fire weapon at his waist confronted me. He asked me if I were a doctor, and I told him I was. He then told me to follow him and he led me through the ER that was normally packed with people but now was entirely empty of patients and staff. We stopped at Trauma Room 1 and I hurried inside. As I passed through the door, I glanced at the clock on the far wall and it indicated it was twenty minutes until one o'clock. In the center of the trauma room and lying on the gurney unclothed was a large man. At that moment I recognized President John F. Kennedy as the man. There was another gurney pushed against the left wall of the room that contained the discarded clothes and suit remnants of the president (they had been cut off him as is standard procedure in such cases). Dr. Jim Carrico, a second year surgery resident, was at the head of the president's cart with an endotracheal tube placed into the president's mouth and throat, trying to resuscitate him by inflating his lungs with oxygen, and was pumping the bag of a respirator in order to do this.

At the head of the table on the president's left was Dr. Charles R. Baxter who was a professor of surgery in the Department of Surgery. On the opposite side of the gurney was Dr. Malcolm O. Perry, also a professor in the department. They were looking at a small round hole in the anterior neck just at or slightly below the cricoid (a bone that helps to support the pharynx). This hole was approximately five to seven millimeters in diameter and was smoothly rounded. It was in the location in front of the trachea where you would normally place an opening in the trachea in the form of a tracheostomy to help a person breathe. Dr. Baxter and Dr. Perry were discussing the meaning of the presence of this hole and at this time Dr. Carrico stated that he was having difficulty ventilating the president and we should probably do a tracheotomy. Dr. Perry asked the nurse for a tracheostomy tray and began to make the incision for the tracheostomy through the small hole and to each side of it so a tube could be inserted directly into the trachea.

In the meantime a nurse was trying to get a blood pressure reading and an intern, Dr. White, was doing a cutdown to insert a catheter in a vein as a route to infuse fluid and medications as needed. I was trying to assess the situation and as far as I could tell, the patient had a massive head injury to the posterior and right occipital-parietal area of the head. His left eye seemed to be slightly bulging also as if there had been a great deal of pressure intra-cranially and perhaps distorting the left eye socket. By palpation, the large area in the back of the head on the right was spongy and covered with matted hair and blood, and I could feel a crepitus or a crackling as I touched the area like the bones were in pieces. This is much like a hard-boiled egg that has been dropped and the shell shattered but still held together by the tissue in the egg and you can feel the pieces of shell grating against one another.

Dr. Carrico was still saying that he could not effectively ventilate the patient and was concerned about a pneumothorax, or a collapse of the lung, and perhaps we should insert a chest tube to try to alleviate the collapse and expand the lung. As I started to make the incision in the right chest to insert the chest tube, Dr. Paul Peters came into the room and as he was part of the surgical staff (urology), he continued with the insertion of the chest tube. At this point in time, the trauma room was beginning to fill up with other residents and staff trying to help but mainly observing and I could see that it may actually impede the resuscitation if it became any more crowded so I left the room to see what else needed to be done.

RIYAD TAHA, MD

On November 22, 1963, I was in my second year of cardiac fellowship, working on emergency room cases that day. Suddenly we got a call that the president was in town, he was shot in the parade downtown, and the motorcade was on their way to Parkland. Everyone was very shocked and immediately we were all given duties to be prepared for when the president came in. I was in charge of bringing the cardiac monitor and pacemaker machine into the room. When they brought him in there was brain tissue all over his wife's clothes. I stood and watched my professors and other doctors trying to do everything they could for him. Apparently the bullet had exploded in his brain, his heartbeat was very slow, and there was no way we could resuscitate him, he may have already been dead when they brought him in. Everyone was very sad; the emergency room was very quiet afterwards.

Charles Baxter, MD

(excerpted from his testimony at the Warren
Commission Hearings)

Mr. SPECTER. And will you outline briefly the circumstances surrounding your being called to render such assistance?

Dr. BAXTER. I was conducting the student health service in the hours of 12 to 1 and was contacted there by the supervisor of the emergency room, who told me that the president was on the way to the emergency room, having been shot.

I went on a dead run to the emergency room as fast as I could and it took me about 3 or 4 minutes to get there. . . .

Mr. SPECTER. When you arrived, what did you observe as to the condition of the president?

Dr. BAXTER. He was very obviously in extremis. There was a large gaping wound in the skull which was covered at that time with blood, and its extent was not immediately determined. His eyes were bulging, the pupils were fixed and dilated and deviated outward, both pupils were deviated laterally. At that time his breathing was being assisted so that whether he was breathing on his own or not, I couldn't determine. . . .

Mr. SPECTER. Who is that who said that [the president still had a heartbeat] to you?

Dr. BAXTER. Well, I believe this was Carrico who said that his heart was still beating. There was present at the time two intravenous catheters in place with fluids running. We were informed at that time—well, having looked over the rest of the body, the only other wound was in his neck, that we saw.

Dr. Carrico said that he had observed a tracheal laceration. At that moment Dr. Jones, I believe, was placing in a left anterior chest tube because of this information. We proceeded at that time with a tracheotomy. . . .

Mr. SPECTER. What else, if anything, did you do for President Kennedy at that time?

Dr. BAXTER. During the tracheotomy, I helped with the insertion of a right anterior chest tube, and then helped Dr. Perry complete the tracheotomy. At that point none of us could hear a heartbeat present. Apparently this had ceased during the tracheotomy and the chest tube placement.

We then gave him or Dr. Perry and Dr. Clark alternated giving him closed chest cardiac massage only until we could get a cardioscope hooked up to tell us if there were any detectible heartbeat electrically present, at least, and there was none, and we discussed at that moment whether we should open the chest to attempt to revive him, while the closed chest massage was going on, and we had an opportunity to look at his head wound then and saw that the damage was beyond hope, that is, in a word—literally the right side of his head had been blown off. With this and the observation that the cerebellum was present—a large quantity of brain was present on the cart, well—we felt that such an additional heroic attempt was not warranted, and we did not pronounce him dead but ceased our efforts, and awaited the priest and Last Rites before we pronounced him dead. . . .

Mr. SPECTER. Will you read into the record, Dr. Baxter, the contents of your report, because it is a little hard to read in spots?

Dr. BAXTER. I was contacted at approximately 12:40 that the president was on the way to the emergency room, having been shot. On arrival there, I found an endotracheal tube in place with assisted respirations, a left chest tube being inserted, and cutdowns going in one leg and in the left arm.

The president had a wound in the midline of the neck. On first observation of the remaining wounds, the temporal and parietal bones were missing and the brain was lying on the table with extensive lacerations and contusions. The pupils were fixed and deviated laterally and dilated. No pulse was detectable, respirations were (as noted) being supplemented. A tracheotomy was performed by Dr. Perry and I and a chest tube inserted into the right chest (second interspace anteriorly). Meanwhile, two pints of O negative blood was administered by pump without response. When all of these measures were complete, no heartbeat could be detected, closed chest massage was performed until a cardioscope could be attached, which revealed no cardiac activity was obtained.

Due to the extensive and irreparable brain damage which was detected, no further attempt to resuscitate the heart was made.

PAUL PETERS, MD

(excerpted from his testimony at the Warren
Commission Hearings)

Mr. SPECTER. Did you have occasion to render medical services to President John Kennedy on November 22, 1963?

Dr. PETERS. Yes.

Mr. SPECTER. And would you outline briefly the circumstances relating to your arriving on the scene where he was?

Dr. PETERS. As I just gave you a while ago?

Mr. SPECTER. Yes.

Dr. PETERS. I was in the adjacent portion of the hospital preparing material for a lecture to the medical students and residents later in the day, when I heard over the radio that the president had been shot and there was a great deal of confusion at the time and the extent of his injuries was not immediately broadcast over the radio, and I thought, because of the description of the location of the tragedy he would probably be brought to Parkland for care, and so I went to the emergency room to see if I could render assistance.

Mr. SPECTER. And at about what time did you arrive at the emergency room?

Dr. PETERS. Well, could I ask a question or two?

Mr. SPECTER. Sure.

Dr. PETERS. As I recall, he was shot about 12:35 our time; is that correct?

Mr. SPECTER. I believe that's been fixed most precisely at 12:30, Dr. Peters.

Dr. PETERS. So, I would estimate it was probably about 12:50 when I got there, I really don't know for certain.

Mr. SPECTER. Whom did you find present, if anyone, when you arrived?

Dr. PETERS. When I arrived the following people I noted were present in the room: Drs. Perry, Baxter, Ron Jones, and McClelland. The first thing I noticed, of course, was that President Kennedy was on the stretcher and that his feet were slightly elevated. He appeared to be placed in a position in which we usually treat a patient who is in shock, and I noticed that Dr. Perry and Dr. Baxter were present and that they were working on his throat. I also noticed that Dr. Ron Jones was present in the room. I took off my coat and asked what I could do to help, and then saw it was President Kennedy. I really didn't know it was President Kennedy until that time. Dr. Perry was there and he and Dr. Baxter were doing the tracheotomy and we asked for a set of tracheotomy tubes to try and get one of the appropriate size. I then helped Dr. Baxter assemble the tracheotomy tube which he inserted into the tracheotomy wound that he and Dr. Perry had created.

Mr. SPECTER. Were there any others present at that time, before you go on as to what aid you rendered?

Dr. PETERS. I believe Dr. Carrico—

Mr. SPECTER. Any other doctors present?

Dr. PETERS. And Dr. Jenkins was present.

Mr. SPECTER. Have you now covered all of those who were present at that time?

Dr. PETERS. And Dr. Shaw walked into the room and left—for a moment—but he didn't stay. He just sort of glanced at the president and went across the hall. Mrs. Kennedy was in the corner with someone who identified himself as the personal physician of the president—I don't remember his name.

Mr. SPECTER. Dr. Burkley?

Dr. PETERS. I don't know his name. That's just who he said he was, because he was asking that the president be given some steroids, which was done.

Mr. SPECTER. He requested that.

Dr. PETERS. That's right, he said he should have some steroids because he was an Addisonian.

Mr. SPECTER. What do you mean by that in lay language?

Dr. PETERS. Well, Addison's disease is a disease of the adrenal cortex which is characterized by a deficiency in the elaboration of certain hormones that allow an individual to respond to stress and these hormones are necessary for life, and if they cannot be replaced, the individual may succumb.

Mr. SPECTER. And Dr. Burkley, or whoever was the president's personal physician, made a request that you treat him as an Addisonian?

Dr. PETERS. That's right—he recommended that he be given steroids because he was an Addisonian—that's what he said. . . .

Mr. SPECTER. Now, tell us what aid was rendered to President Kennedy.

Dr. PETERS. Dr. Perry and Dr. Baxter were doing the tracheotomy and a set of tracheotomy tubes was obtained and the appropriate size was determined and I gave it to Baxter, who helped Perry put it into the wound, and Perry noted also that there appeared to be a bubbling sensation in the chest and recommended that chest tubes be put in. Dr. Ron Jones put a chest tube in on the left side and Dr. Baxter and I put it in on the right side—I made the incision in the president's chest, and I noted that there was no bleeding from the wound.

Mr. SPECTER. Did you put that chest tube all the way in on the right side?

Dr. PETERS. That's our presumption—yes.

Mr. SPECTER. And what else was done for the president?

Dr. PETERS. About the same time—there was a question of whether he really had an adequate pulse, and so Dr. Ronald Jones and I pulled his pants down and noticed that he was wearing his brace which had received a lot of publicity in the lay press, and also that he had an elastic bandage wrapped around his pelvis at— in a sort of a figure eight fashion, so as to encompass both thighs and the lower trunk.

Mr. SPECTER. What was the purpose of that bandage?

Dr. PETERS. I presume that it was—my thoughts at the time were that he probably had been having pelvic pain and had put this on as an additional support to stabilize his lower pelvis. It seemed quite interesting to me that the president of the United States had on an ordinary $3 Ace bandage probably in an effort to stabilize his pelvis. I suppose he had been having some back pain and that was my thought at the time, but we removed this bandage in an effort to feel a femoral pulse. We were never certain that we got a good pulse. . . .

Mr. SPECTER. [The brace was running] in his waist area at the top of his hips up to the lower part of his chest?

Dr. PETERS. I would estimate that it went from the lower part of his chest to the pelvic girdle. About this time it was noted also that he had no effective heart action, and Dr. Perry asked whether he should open the chest and massage the heart. In the meantime, of course, the tracheotomy had been done and completed and had been hooked on to apparatus for assisting his respiration.

Mr. SPECTER. And what action, if any, was taken on the open-heart massage?

Dr. PETERS. It was pointed out that an examination of the brain had been done. Dr. Jenkins had observed the brain and Dr. Clark had observed the brain and it was pointed out to Dr. Perry that it appeared to be a mortal wound, and involving the brain, and that open-heart massage would probably not add anything to what had already been done, and that external cardiac massage is known to be as efficient as direct massage of the heart itself.

Mr. SPECTER. Was there any further treatment rendered to the president?

Dr. PETERS. Yes, Dr. Perry began immediate external compression of the chest in an effort to massage the heart, even before he asked the question as to whether the thoracotomy should be done. As soon as there was a question as to whether there was a pulse or not, he immediately began external chest compression.

Mr. SPECTER. What other action was taken to aid the president, if any?

Dr. PETERS. Well, cutdowns were done on the extremities, and tubes were inserted in the veins, and I know on the right ankle anteriorly, and I believe in the left arm and also in the left leg, in order to administer fluid and blood which he did receive.

Mr. SPECTER. Have you now described all of the medical attention given the president?

Dr. PETERS. Well, I believe I have.

Mr. SPECTER. And was the president subsequently pronounced dead?

Dr. PETERS. That's correct.

Mr. SPECTER. And about what time was that pronouncement made?

Dr. PETERS. I could not give you the time within five or ten minutes—I can tell you this much, though, I know what actually did happen.

Mr. SPECTER. Tell me that.

Dr. PETERS. I was—we pronounced him dead and I was in the room, present while the priest gave him the last rites, during which time there was Dr. Jenkins and Dr. Baxter and Dr. McClelland, Mrs. Kennedy, the priest, and myself. Dr. Perry had left, as had most of the others by that time.

RON JONES, MD

(from *Baylor Reflections,* November 22, 1998)

I called the operator asking why so many stat pages for department chairmen and she said, "The president has been shot and they're bringing him to the emergency room and need physicians."

Dr. Malcolm Perry and I, along with Red Duke, one of the junior residents, took the back steps down one flight to the emergency room. Dr. Perry and I went to Trauma Room 1 and Dr. Duke to Trauma Room 2.

As we entered the room, the president was already on a cart, motionless, his eyes open with a stare. Mrs. Kennedy was standing in the corner near the doorway. Dr. Jim Carrico, a second year resident was attempting to intubate the president and two junior residents were attempting to start an intravenous line. It was obvious the president was not breathing although Dr. Carrico thought he had seen agonal respirations. There was a small wound in the midline of the lower neck, less than 1 cm. and a posterior head injury on the right.

Dr. Perry immediately started performing a tracheotomy and I performed a cutdown on the cephalic vein of the left arm. . . . I inserted a left anterior chest tube in the second interspace in the mid-clavicular line. Dr. Paul Peters, Dr. Charles Baxter, who had been helping Dr. Perry with the tracheotomy—with some assistance from me—inserted a right chest tube. A portable EKG machine was moved into the room and a tracing obtained on the president revealed a straight line.

I left the room and was quickly greeted by a Secret Service agent and asked, "What is the condition of the president? I need to phone Joseph Kennedy and tell him the condition of his son." Within a few steps, I was also greeted by someone from the Federal Bureau of Investigation who asked the same question and stated, "I have to call J. Edgar Hoover and inform him of the condition of the president."

At that moment, no announcement of the president's condition had been made. The agents were unable to get an outside telephone line since all phones were blocked by incoming calls, which would soon be coming from all over the world. I took them to the telephone switchboard operator in an attempt for her to obtain an outside line.

We went down the back steps and went into Trauma Room 1, which was just across the hall from Trauma Room 2 where Governor Connally had been taken. The president was already in the room and apparently had just arrived perhaps seconds or a minute before we arrived in the trauma room. And very quickly— and I mean, within a minute or so—that room literally filled with physicians, both residents and attending staff. As you entered the trauma room, the emergency room supervisor, Doris Nelson, was on one side of the door, and there was a policeman on the opposite side. And they were trying to determine who needed to come into that room, but that was very difficult without knowing what the injuries were because many of these physicians represented different specialties.

Ideally, you would not have that room so crowded, but they did not know who to keep out and who to let in. And as a result, many, many people came into that room to the point that you literally could not move around the room to get to . . . directly to supplies. It was a relatively small room. It had a stretcher in the middle of it, and there was probably five feet, six feet on each side of that stretcher. And the same distance at the head and maybe a little more at the foot. And as we entered the room, Mrs. Kennedy was standing in the corner of the room to my left as I entered the room.

Dr. Malcom Perry was a young staff man at that time. I was chief resident under him, and when we went into that room together, he was the senior person in that room. And so he took charge of the president's room. Dr. Duke apparently went into Governor Connally's room as a resident, and I think from there, Dr. Robert Shaw was contacted, who was a well-known thoracic surgeon. And Dr. Shaw seemed to take charge then of Governor Connally. That probably took a few minutes to establish that relationship. As other people came in the room, some of them were residents and some were young attending staff at that time. But I think that Dr. Perry seemed to be the one in charge of the president's room.

Dr. Jenkins came down just a short time later. Dr. James Carrico was already in the room when we entered to look at the president.

I didn't pay any attention to the police at that time other than to know that they were there. They did not have any obstacles as far as the treatment. And I really didn't appreciate the presence of the FBI and the Secret Service until I walked out of the room. At that point, we were so focused on what we were doing that we, I think . . . at least I didn't pay much attention to who was around me other than I just knew a lot of people were in the room. And sort of felt the awesome responsibility that these people had.

I think very quickly we determined who was going to do what. As I looked at the president, I didn't see him move at all. I personally did not see any respiration activity or attempt at respiration. The eyes, as I recall, were open but staring straight ahead without any motion. I did not [shaking head] take the blood pressure, nor did I listen to a heartbeat. I think what triggered the resuscitative effort was that Dr. Carrico had thought that he had seen some agonal respiration at the time the president arrived.

I knew that he was not breathing. And I talked to Dr. Perry very quickly, and I said, "We probably need to do a trach and get a cutdown or access to a vein to get an IV started." [nodding] And one of us—or both of us simultaneously—said that doctor . . . that Malcolm would do the tracheotomy, and I would do the cutdown in the left arm, which is just making an incision in the skin, isolating or finding a vein and getting a catheter into the vein. So, he started on the tracheotomy, and I started on the cutdown. Dr. Carrico was at the head of the table, I recall, and he was attempting to place a tube into the throat or into the trachea and in the tracheal tube to establish an airway.

Occasionally, you will see a trauma patient come in and . . . who has just arrested or had their heart stop, and maybe if their injuries are not severe—so severe as this was—you can immediately start resuscitation and bring them back. And we thought maybe that was a possibility. When I went down there, I had assumed that he had probably been shot in the stomach or the chest, and that he was OK. Or he had been shot in the arm. It was just a matter of taking care of him, of taking him to the operating room if need be, and he was going to be all right. And it wasn't until I went into the Trauma Room 1 that I realized the [nodding] seriousness of this injury. Most of the gunshot wounds that we saw at that time were relatively low caliber—.22, .32, occasional .38 caliber injuries. And that was because most people were shot with small handguns or stabs . . . stab wounds and so forth occurred. So, we didn't see a lot of high velocity injuries, as far as the method of injury is concerned.

But as we worked on the president for a little bit, we realized that there was a head wound, but even then, we hadn't had time to assess the severity of that injury. And were still working for the first two or three minutes [smiling and nodding] with the idea that maybe there was a possibility of resuscitating the president. But that doubt [nodding] dissipated fairly quickly as we got started.

As Dr. Perry made the tracheotomy incision, and I made the cutdown incision, those two procedures were going along reasonably well and reasonably quickly. I'd . . . I could not reach the cutdown tray—or the venous section tray, as it was called—which was just a matter of six or eight feet away from me because of the number of people that were in the room. And one of the nurses handed me the tray which had the knife and the catheter in it to perform . . . and the [word indecipherable] to perform a cutdown to establish an IV. And I couldn't get to gloves, and so I did the cutdown barehanded and just quickly made an incision. I could see the vein right here in his left arm and then took the catheter and threaded it very quickly into the vein, and we got IV fluids going immediately.

About the time I had finished that, Dr. Perry was doing the tracheostomy . . . performing the tracheostomy with Dr. Charles Baxter, and they thought they heard a gush of air come from the neck. And they didn't know whether there could have been an injury to the chest through this neck wound, and perhaps the lung had collapsed. And so, I asked Dr. Perry, "Do you want to have a chest tube placed?" And he said, "Yes." And so, I then made a . . . got another tray to insert a chest tube and made a short incision in the left front chest just below the collarbone about two or three finger breadths and placed a trocar and then put a chest tube in place. And as I recall, Dr. Carrico had come around to that side of the table at that time. He was, I believe, a second-year resident, and he put the tube into the water suction bottle, which was the method that we used of expanding a pneumothorax if that happened to be the case at that time. And we did not get any blood at that time, nor did we see any air bubbling.

Not knowing which side that might have occurred on, we went to the left side and because I couldn't go around the table and Dr. Paul Peters, the chairman of urology, was on that side of the table. He had come into the room by that time, and Dr. Baxter was at the head of the table performing the tracheotomy with Dr. Perry. So, Perry and I were on the president's left, Dr. Peters and Dr. Baxter were on the president's right side. So, the three of us sort of put in the chest tube in the right side.

By the time we had done that, we had an EKG—a portable electrocardiogram—brought into the room and leads were placed on the chest. And all we had on the tracing was just a straight line, so there was no heart activity. There was no heartbeat. And I think from the time we walked into the room until that time was probably no more than ten minutes. We thought that we came . . . I thought that we came in the room about twenty-five minutes until 1:00. And within ten minutes, the tracheotomy had been performed. Dr. Jenkins and Dr. Carrico had the tracheal tube in. We had chest tubes in. We had the cutdown going, IV fluid going, and probably another IV going in the lower extremity—in the lower leg.

And then, Dr. Perry and Dr. Jenkins and by then Dr. Kemp Clark had come in the room, as I recall. They could look at the head wound a little better, and they could see the extensive injury to the brain. And that's when it really became apparent that there was no use in attempting any additional effort to save his [life] because, number one, there was no evidence that he had been alive during the time that he had been in the emergency room that I could tell or that Dr. Perry, I think, could tell, and with that type of injury, you were almost certain that even if he did have a heart-beat, he could not maintain life with that degree of brain injury. I could not look up over the head because I was down at this level of the body and could not see over the head back here [indicating top and back of head] as he was flat on the cart, to see the extensive head injury that he apparently had, at least enough to get a real accurate description of what that injury looked like or the size of the defect that that missile had caused.

We didn't turn him over either because Mrs. Kennedy was in the room. He obviously had expired. And we felt at the time because of . . . perhaps of her presence that we didn't want to appear to be inquisitive or overly inquisitive, and yet in retrospect, that obviously should have been done. And he should have been looked at both front, back—detail measurements made of everything. But as I said at the beginning, we had never witnessed an assassination before, and I think even then, we did not appreciate the impact that this had already had on the world. And that came to light as I walked out of the room at about fifteen minutes until 1:00 or so.

When we stopped performing any additional procedures on the president, we still were not totally sure that all was lost and very quickly, the question came up, should we open his chest and try to do open heart massage? And I think, at that point, you have decide[d] is this something that you want to do? Do you want to do any more surgery on someone who has no chance of living? She's in the room, and that question briefly surfaced. And I think the decision was that with the extent of the brain injury that we might do some closed chest massage, which had become fairly popular at that . . . shortly before that period of time. And Dr. Perry started closed chest massage. We thought that we needed to cut the clothes off to see if we were getting a palatable pulse, and as I recall, we cut the coat, shirt, and the trousers off without trying to lift him up and take it off. So, we cut the clothes away, and that was when we noticed the Ace bandage wrapped around the abdomen, the stomach, and the back, which . . . apparently he had a back brace and went down one leg. And so, I tried to feel for a pulse to see if the closed chest massage was effective, and we also got the word at that time that Mrs. Kennedy, I think, wanted a priest called and that we probably were not to pronounce him until the priest arrived. And in the meantime, I think Dr. Carrico had administered some steroids IV, and that was about the time that I walked out. Whoever spoke to Mrs. Kennedy—and I did not—did so after I left the room.

Robert McClelland, MD

(from *D Magazine*, November 2008)

The first thing he saw was the president's face, cyanotic— bluish-black, swollen, suffused with blood. The body was on a cart in the middle of the room, draped and surrounded by doctors and residents. Kennedy was completely motionless, a contrast to the commotion around him. McClelland was relieved there were so many other faculty members there. . . .

McClelland put on surgical gloves. None of the men in the room had changed clothes. At their wrists, the surgical gloves met business suits and pressed white shirt cuffs.

Jenkins had his hands full, but nodded down to Kennedy's head. He said, "Bob, there's a wound there." The head was covered in blood and blood clots, tiny collections of dark red mass. McClelland thought he meant there was a wound at the president's left temple. Later that gesture would cause some confusion.

McClelland moved to the head of the cart. "Bob, would you hold this retractor?" Perry asked. He handed McClelland an army-navy retractor, a straight metal bar with curves on each end to hold back tissue and allow visibility and access. McClelland leaned over the president's blue face, over the gape in the back of his head, and took the tool.

For nearly 15 minutes, McClelland held the retractor as blood ran over its edges. As the other doctors labored on Kennedy's throat and chest or milled around the room, McClelland stood staring at the leader of the free world. His face was 18 inches from the president's head wound. Kennedy's eyes bulged slightly from their sockets—the medical term is "protuberant"—common with massive head injuries and increased intracranial pressure. Blood oozed down his cheeks. Some of the hair at the front of his head was still combed.

McClelland looked into the head wound. Stray hairs at the back of the head covered parts of the hole, as did bits of bone, blood, and more blood clots. He watched as a piece of cerebellum slowly slipped from the back of the hole and dropped onto the cart.

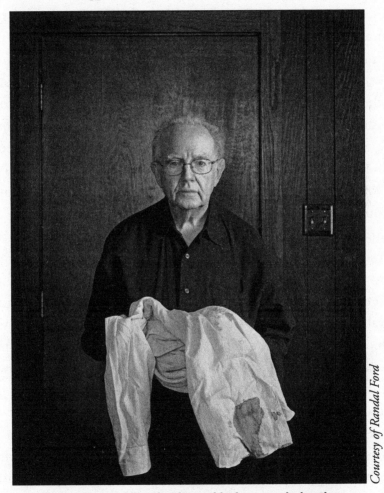

Courtesy of Randal Ford

Shown here holding the dress shirt he wore during the resuscitation effort, Dr. McClelland has preserved this bloodstained artifact for posterity. Still teaching at the age of eighty-four, he is a treasure of Southwestern Medical School.

ROBERT MCCLELLAND, MD

(oral history courtesy of the Sixth Floor Musuem)

A huge big crowd just filled the emergency room. And I thought, "Well, something's going on here." And then the crowd parted enough that I saw Mrs. Kennedy sitting there on a chair in that famous pink suit, and I thought, "Oh my God." And at that point, see, I knew Dr. Shires was in Galveston at a meeting. I didn't know where anybody else was, and here I was [chuckling], a thirty-four-year-old instructor in surgery and here I may be . . . maybe I'm it, for all I knew. And I had to almost force myself to not turn around and run and to keep going back toward that room, you know. And Doris Nelson, who was the head nurse in there, was telling people, you know, the Secret Service, who to let by, and so she said, "Let him by, he's one of the doctors." And I went on into the room, the rear of the room, but that meant that I saw his face, and as I came in, that was the first vivid impression I got. So, I walked on around to the . . . between the gurney he was lying on and the wall and walked up toward the head of the gurney where Dr. Jenkins was, and they had . . . and Dr. Carrico had intubated him, and they had him hooked up to an anesthesia machine, and Dr. Perry, who was standing out there when I arrived today, and Dr. Baxter had started doing a tracheotomy on the president.

And so, I didn't see anything I could do, but I went up to the head of the gurney, and they seemed to be having a little difficulty seeing, and so I said, "Well, here, let me hold the retractor for you." And I took a . . . what we call a metal . . . a so-called Army/Navy retractor, just a little straight piece of metal, and it was retracting the upper edge of the tracheal incision, leaning over the president's head doing that. So, I had not much to do other than that. While they continued the tracheotomy and everybody else was running around in the room,

I stood there for, I guess ten or fifteen minutes, looking right into the head wound. And as I stood there, you know, part of the cerebellum fell out on the . . . on the cart there. And I knew that I thought to myself . . . I still remember thinking, "Well, gee, that's part of the cerebellum." And of course, Pepper Jenkins said that in his original testimony, but he denied later that he said it, even though it was in the record, and that it was cerebral tissue. Well, it wasn't cerebral tissue, it was cerebellar tissue, and I'm as certain of that as my name, even though that was not apparently thought to be the case later. I know it was, and so anyway, this hole that I was looking at . . . I could sit here now and almost draw it in detail for you, thirty-some odd years later because I looked at it and I was that far from it [holding hands a few inches from his face]. Everybody else was just kind of moving around catching glimpses of it, and I was sort of burning it into my visual field.

You're just reacting. You're not really thinking about, well, what am I going to do next? You're just kind of going from one immediate impression to the next. It's a moment of reactions, not thoughts and reactions and . . . and, of course, I think the immediate reaction was that once he's pronounced dead, it was none of our business. That we then weren't, you know, going to go over him carefully because it was clear that they wanted . . . everybody wanted to get out of there, and so you didn't delay anything. And we, in fact, almost everybody left the room . . . the doctors. The only two people that were left in there were Dr. Baxter and myself, and the president's body and the reason we were still in there is that before we could get out of the room where we happened to be standing when he was pronounced dead. We were, again, between the gurney and the wall, and about the time that Dr. Baxter and I were gonna walk around that head of the gurney and leave the room behind everybody else, the door came open and Father Hubert came in, and we'd almost have to knock him down or push him out of the way to get out of the way, so we just kind of melted back up against the wall. And so, he came in then, you know, and put his little thing around his neck, and we stood there while he gave the president his Last Rites.

KEMP CLARK, MD

(excerpted from his testimony at the Warren
Commission Hearings)

Mr. SPECTER. What did you observe the president's condition to be on your arrival there?

Dr. CLARK. The president was lying on his back on the emergency cart. Dr. Perry was performing a tracheotomy. There were chest tubes being inserted. Dr. Jenkins was assisting the president's respirations through a tube in his trachea. Dr. Jones and Dr. Carrico were administering fluids and blood intravenously. The president was making a few spasmodic respiratory efforts. I assisted in withdrawing the endotracheal tube from the throat as Dr. Perry was then ready to insert the tracheotomy tube. I then examined the president briefly. My findings showed his pupils were widely dilated, did not react to light, and his eyes were deviated outward with a slight skew deviation.

I then examined the wound in the back of the president's head. This was a large, gaping wound in the right posterior part, with cerebral and cerebellar tissue being damaged and exposed. There was considerable blood loss evident on the carriage, the floor, and the clothing of some of the people present. I would estimate 1,500 cc. of blood being present.

As I was examining the president's wound, I felt for a carotid pulse and felt none. Therefore, I began external cardiac massage and asked that a cardiotachioscope be connected. Because of my position it was difficult to administer cardiac massage. However, Dr. Jones stated that he felt a femoral pulse.

Mr. SPECTER. What did the cardiotachioscope show at that time?

Dr. CLARK. By this time the cardiotachioscope, we just call it a cardiac monitor for a better word. . . .

Mr. SPECTER. That's a good word.

Dr. CLARK. The cardiotachioscope had been attached and Dr. Fouad Bashour had arrived. There was transient electrical activity of the president's heart of an undefined type. Approximately, at this time the external cardiac massage became ineffectual and no pulsations could be felt. At this time it was decided to pronounce the president dead.

Mr. SPECTER. At what time was this fixed?

Dr. CLARK. Death was fixed at 1 p.m.

Mr. SPECTER. Was that a precise time or an approximate time, or in what way did you fix the time of death at one o'clock?

Dr. CLARK. This was an approximation as it is, first, extremely difficult to stage precisely when death occurs. Secondly, no one was monitoring the clock, so an approximation of one o'clock was chosen.

Mr. SPECTER. Who was it who actually fixed the time of death?

Dr. CLARK. I did.

MICHAEL ELLSASSER, MD

Don Gilliard and I went to the ER cubicle where they had attempted resuscitation and pronounced the president dead. The room had yet to be cleaned and Jackie Kennedy's bouquet of blood spattered roses rested in a waste can. Don and I each took a rose, and later had them encased in plastic. They didn't come out very well, but I still have that piece of history.

Courtesy of the Parkland Health and Hospital System

The door to Trauma Room 1 bore this wreath for many days after our president died there.

CHAPTER 7

MEMORIES OF THE FIRST LADY

The Secret Service and hospital personnel tried to prevent Jackie Kennedy from entering Trauma Room 1, but she jerked free from their restraining hands, saying, "I'm just as competent as you are." An article in the *Journal of the American Medical Association* published three decades later reports the searing memories of Pepper Jenkins, the chief of anesthesiology, who was ventilating the president during the frantic resuscitation effort.

Norman Borge was working in the psychiatric emergency room adjacent to the Pit when the dying president was brought into the ER. Seeing Jackie standing in the doorway of Trauma Room 1, Borge found her a chair in which she sat rigidly, her hands folded in her lap. She seemed to him to be "staring at the crowd without seeing them." He thought to do the human thing by bringing her a cup of water. When he handed it to Jackie, she smiled at him and said, "Thank you very much, I appreciate it." Borge's memories of the First Lady were published in the *Fort Worth Star-Telegram* in 1965 and they tell of her remarkable graciousness during the worst moments of her life.

On that fateful day in November, 1963, I was a young first year resident at Parkland Memorial Hospital. Having been on duty the night before, I was asleep in the second floor room provided for residents. Suddenly I was awakened by a lot of loud noise and confusion and people around. I asked someone what was happening and they said the President had just been brought into Emergency. Still in my scrubs, I headed for the Emergency area. Just as I arrived there, Mrs. Kennedy came out of Trauma Room 1. She passed very close to me, and to this day, my most vivid and terrible memory of that day is the sight of the beautiful First Lady, her stricken look, her clothes spattered with the President's blood.

Jimmie Shiu M.D.

Jimmie Shiu, M.D.
Class of 1961

蕭復旦

ROBERT DUCHOUQUETTE, MD

The whole nation cried, the day I met JFK. During my lunch hour that sunny autumn day, November 22, 1963, the youngest man ever to be elected as president of the United States was visiting Dallas, where I was a junior medical student at the University of Texas Southwestern Medical School. I was in my car, wearing my OB-GYN scrubs, on the way to get a sandwich, only three blocks from Parkland Hospital. As I approached the stoplight on Harry Heinz Boulevard, three limousines careened around the corner, streaking northward toward the hospital, escorted by a bevy of police motorcycles. In the center of the back seat of the second limousine of the trio, Jackie Kennedy was pressed into its cushions, partially shielded and held upright by a Secret Service agent sprawled across the trunk. Jack was lying diagonally across her, from her waist to her shoulder, his head bloodied by the recent assault, as she held him.

M. T. "PEPPER" JENKINS, MD

(excerpted from the *Journal of the American Medical Association*, May 1992)

. . . I was standing with the front of my jacket against his head wound, an alignment that put me in the best position to carry out artificial ventilation. I was getting gushes of blood down my jacket and into my shoes. Jackie Kennedy was circling the room, walking behind my back. The Secret Service could not keep her out of the room. She looked shell shocked. As she circled and circled, I noticed her hands were cupped in front of her, as if she were cradling something. As she passed by, she nudged me with an elbow and handed me what she had been nursing with her hands—a large chunk of her husband's brain tissue. I quickly handed it to a nurse.

WILLIAM ZEDLITZ, MD

Just outside the trauma room door, Mrs. Jacqueline Kennedy was sitting in a folding metal chair, dressed in a watermelon colored suit dress that was liberally spotted with darker splotches of red, along with bits of whitish tissue that represented the spray from the president's head wound. I stopped and asked her if she would like to wait somewhere a little quieter and more private but she thanked me and said she would rather wait here until she knew the outcome of the resuscitation.

ADEL NAFRAWI, MD

It was lunch time when we heard the chiefs of services called "stat" to the ER, including the late Dr. Fouad Bashour. We had heard that President Kennedy was shot. I took the elevator down and as the doors opened I was confronted by two armed officers. I went to the room where the president lay. Dr. Kemp Clark, Dr. Perry and others were there and in the corner was Mrs. Kennedy in the now famous blood spattered dress.

Then somebody called for a defibrillator so I went to the lab and wheeled in the refrigerator-size defibrillator. By that time Dr. Clark had called off the code. This is when Mrs. Kennedy moved toward the president, removed the wedding ring from his hand, kissed him and put the ring on her finger.

On my way back I encountered the priest wondering where to go. I said, "That way, Father," and showed him the room. God— those images are as vivid today as on that day.

M.T. "PEPPER" JENKINS, MD

(excerpted from the *Journal of the American Medical Association*, May 1992)

By this time, the Secret Service had allowed a catholic priest to enter the room to administer the Last Rites. All of the medical staff seemed to disappear, dissolve, fade from the room, except, I believe, for me and Dr. Baxter. I was busy disconnecting the electrocardiographic leads, removing the IVs and extracting the endotracheal tube. However, before I could finish these duties, Mrs. Kennedy returned to the president's side and I retreated to a corner of the room. She kissed the president on the foot, on the leg, on the thigh, on the abdomen, on the chest, and then on the face. She still looked drawn, pale, shocked and remote. I doubt if she remembers any part of this. Then the priest began the Last Rites in deliberate, resonant and slow tones and then it was over.

NORMAN BORGE, MD

(excerpted from the *Fort Worth Star-Telegram*, November 1965)

The First Lady, her bright pink suit marred by the darker stain of blood, was helped from the treatment room by two agents. In frenzy, she freed her arms and wrenched away from them. "I'm just as capable as you are!" Dr. Borge heard her say.

But she didn't say a thing as she sat by the door in a chair provided her by Borge. She only stared at the crowd without really seeing them, he recalled.

What really struck him, he said, was her graciousness when he offered her a drink of water. "She sat there rigidly, her hands clasped in her lap," Dr. Borge said, "and I didn't notice her looking at me because I was trying to keep the water from spilling."

But when he glanced at her face, she smiled broadly and said, "Thank you very much. I appreciate it"

"How, could anyone conjure up such a gracious appearance after what had happened?" Dr. Borge speculated.

When the bronze-trimmed brown metal coffin was pushed into the room, Mrs. Kennedy followed it with her eyes. "Her attention seemed to focus on the immediate presence of the president's body," Dr. Borge observed. "She communicated to no one except to be gracious." Dr. Borge watched as the First Lady followed the casket bearing her husband's body outside, on her way to the swearing in of the new president

In that brief space of time, his life had touched a great national tragedy at its roots. They would be planted in his mind forever.

RON JONES, MD

(oral history courtesy of the Sixth Floor Museum)

My impression when I saw her was that she was very composed under the circumstances. And she appeared to be in a situation where she knew that this could happen, it had happened, and she realized this, and she was ready to accept this. It seemed as though she was almost prepared mentally that something like this could take place. I'm sure she was shocked by this, but she was holding up very well emotionally. And as I said, it just seemed as though she knew that this could happen. It had happened.

ROBERT MCCLELLAND, MD

(oral history courtesy of the Sixth Floor Museum)

As he [the priest] took his little cloth off his neck and was putting his things back in his little bag, after having anointed the president and whatnot, she came in and leaned over and asked him . . . and we could hear her because, again, we were still trapped back there. We felt like we were intruding, but there was no way we could get out without knocking both her and Father Hubert down. And she said, "Have you given him the Last Rites?" And he said, "I've given him conditional Last Rites." She grimaced a little bit then, as if she didn't much like to hear that. And . . . but that's what he had done. I heard . . . I'm not a Catholic, but he leaned over to him and, as I recall, the first thing he did was anoint his forehead with oil, and he said, "If thou livest . . ." Those were the first words he said, and then he went through, you know, the rest of the thing. And he did it in English. You know, that was around the time I think that they shifted from the Latin . . . at least, a lot of them did.

So, she, you know, after that, she kind of stood there for a minute, and she took a ring off and put it on his finger. I can't remember which finger. I don't know. It was a ring, that's all I can say. And she put it on one of his fingers, and I don't know which one she took it off of and which one she put it on, and then she turned and walked slowly out of the room. And as . . . his foot . . . he had already been covered up with a sheet at that time, and his foot was sticking out . . . his right foot was sticking out from underneath the sheet and the lower leg. And as she passed by, she kind of, almost as an afterthought, she leaned over and kissed his foot, and then she walked out of the room. That was it.

KEMP CLARK, MD

(excerpted from his testimony at the Warren
Commission Hearings)

Mr. SPECTER. Did you advise anyone else in the presidential party of the death of the president?

Dr. CLARK. Yes; I told Mrs. Kennedy, the president's wife, of his death.

Mr. SPECTER. And what, if anything, did she respond to you?

Dr. CLARK. She told me that she knew it and thanked me for our efforts.

Courtesy of the Dallas Morning News

Still wearing the bloodstained pink suit, the First Lady, no longer the First Lady, enters the hearse bearing the mortal remains of the thirty-fifth president of the United States.

Chapter 8

WHAT DID KEMP CLARK SAY?

William Kemp Clark, MD, chairman of neurosurgery, was from an aristocratic, "old Dallas" family. My friend, Dr. Barry Silberg, rented the garage apartment of the family's north Dallas estate. I knew Clark because he had been assigned to be my faculty advisor, and I met with him once or twice a year. One on one, he seemed friendly and relaxed, though I know his ferocity in the operating room led some to call him "The Cobra." For the rest of us, his name being so close to Clark Kent, mild mannered reporter for the *Metropolitan Daily News,* that we called him "Man Super."

There are almost as many reports of what Clark said when he called off the resuscitation as there are of his location when the news flashed through the hospital. Wherever he was, it was he who initiated closed chest cardiac massage. There were several reports I received of statements overheard by Jackie such as, "My God, Charlie! What are you doing? His brains are all over the table."

The Parkland Hospital *Our Heritage* collection quotes Clark as having said, "My God, the whole right side of his head is shot off. We've nothing to work with."

After someone relieved Clark of the chest compressions, and he was able to see the devastating defect in the cranial vault and the exposed brain tissue, he may well have said something more forceful than, "There's nothing more to be done."

KEN WALLACE, M.D

Carrico told me a few days later that Clark said, "Goddamit Carrico, what are you doing? Can't you see his brains are blown out?" Jackie, sitting outside the open door, heard the comment.

ADEL NAFRAWI, MD

I went to the room where the president lay. Dr. Kemp Clark, Dr. Perry and others were there and in the corner was Mrs. Kennedy, in the now famous blood spattered dress. "Come on, you guys, you see head injuries every day," sounded Dr. Clark to the medical people taking care of the president.

REX COLE, MD

I heard that heroic measures were being utilized to try to save the president when Kemp Clark arrived, picked up the president's head, saw the exit wound and said something like, "Why are you wasting your time?"

Joe D. Goldstrich, MD

Clark arrived about four minutes after me. He said, "My God, Charlie, what are you doing? His brains are all over the table." This was overheard by Jackie Kennedy.

M.T. "Pepper" Jenkins, MD

(from the *Journal of the American Medical Association*, May 1992)

> *It was Kemp Clark, a Parkland Hospital neurosurgeon, who most closely observed Kennedy's massive head wound. He told Perry, "It's too late, Mac. There's nothing more to be done."*
>
> *It was Clark who pronounced the president dead at 1:00 p.m., only 25 minutes after he was wheeled into the emergency room.*

CHAPTER 9

THE SECRET SERVICE

After nearly five decades of silence, the Secret Service agents who were guarding the president that November day have spoken. Their book, *The Kennedy Detail*, by Agent Gerald Blaine, includes the account of Agent Clint Hill who was ten feet from JFK when he, ". . . heard the first shot, saw the president grab his throat, lurch to the left." Hill was "desperately trying to throw his body in front of the gunfire, when the president's head exploded before his eyes. Covered with blood and pieces of the president's brain, Agent Hill pushed Jackie Kennedy into the back seat, while clinging to the trunk of the open-top limousine as it sped away from Dealey Plaza to Parkland Hospital."

Classmates Cervando Martinez and David Haymes, from their vantage point near the Trade Mart, saw Agent Hill on the trunk, as the sirens wailed and the motorcade raced toward the hospital. Moments later, Agent Hill, his white shirt bloodstained, asked a senior medical student which loading dock door led to the emergency room.

Many reports I received recall the clamor and chaos of the ER, and how the Secret Service struggled for control of the unfamiliar setting. After they established a perimeter, Bill Scroggie saw a man try to push his way past without identifying himself, and the Secret Service agent, "flattened the guy. I later learned he was an FBI agent," Scroggie said.

No one had ever seen guns drawn in the Parkland ER. Dr. Earl Rose, who was the Dallas County Medical Examiner, faced one when he tried to enforce Texas law. Ironically the most intense scene of these historic moments was after the president died. Though Rose made it abundantly clear the body could not be moved until an autopsy was performed, the Secret Service, weapons in evidence, pushed past him. This spiriting away of the body destroyed the chain of evidence, and gave rise to many conspiracy theories.

BILL SCROGGIE, MD

On the day President Kennedy was shot, I was a senior medical student and my duty station was the ER. I was eating lunch in the cafeteria with a classmate of mine when someone waved at us from the window that overlooked the loading dock for the ER. We went over and looked out and there was the Lincoln convertible that the president had been in. So far no news had spread about the shooting.

I knew it was the president's car, so I raced down the back stairs to the back door of the ER. There was a well-dressed man guarding the door (presumed Secret Service) and another fellow tried to push his way through without identifying himself. The Secret Service agent flattened the guy. I later learned it was an FBI agent.

I was in scrubs and he let me go in.

H. WAYNE SMITH, MD

I talked with Jim Carrico a couple of days later. He related how terrified everyone was in the emergency room—personnel and patients—because the Secret Service agents had pretty well lost it and were brandishing firearms and talking/shouting loudly. Jim related how the law enforcement agencies set up the perimeters around the emergency room with Secret Service closest and next the FBI. One FBI agent approached the inner perimeter manned by the Secret Service and was told to halt—the FBI agent responded that he was FBI and kept walking—the Secret Service agent cold-cocked him right there in the hall. It was a wonder he did not get shot. It was a sad day indeed.

WAYNE DELANEY, MD

I was out of town assisting a surgeon in Frederick, Oklahoma doing surgery on my cousin when the event happened. I was interviewed later by the Secret Service or the FBI because of a comment attributed to me on that fateful day. It was their understanding that I had said when everyone entered the ER that all hell broke loose and there were guns drawn and people hitting the floor. They were a little reluctant to believe me saying I was out of town. There was a resident in the ER named George DeVaney, and I believe that was the mix-up. I have a faint recollection that it was still in error in the Warren Report.

RON JONES, MD

(oral history courtesy of the Sixth Floor Museum)

I think twice during the winter months the Secret Service came through. I remember once, I think, the Secret Service out of San

Francisco came through and asked to meet with me, and they asked me if I had any other notes about what went on that day scribbled anywhere that I had not turned in. And I told them that I had written my brief notes and had turned them in to Mr. Jack Price, who was the hospital administrator. He was out of town that day. They indicated they didn't have my notes and that they might be in his safe in his office. Dr. Kemp Clark had put together what he called "Dr. Clark's Summary" and we thought that maybe he had taken some of our handwritten notes and had summarized them and submitted them to the Warren Commission because they said they didn't have them. I think subsequently . . . that they were found. And . . . because I've seen them since, and they're stamped "top secret" [smiling], which is sort of interesting, too [Bob Porter chuckles in the background]. So, they came twice, and it wasn't until the spring when I received a letter from the President's Commission on the Assassination of President Kennedy that—that was in March of 1964—that they were going to be in town two days later and would like to meet with me at Parkland Hospital. So, we were five or six months from the time of the assassination until my deposition was taken for the Warren Commission.

EARL ROSE, MD, AS RECALLED BY JAMES CARRICO, MD

(oral history courtesy of the Sixth Floor Museum)

I was a little surprised in a professional sense and kind of in this sense. As I said, what would usually have happened when a patient would come in and then die of a gunshot wound. We would have tried to keep him alive, we would have done all we needed to do medically, we probably would have spent more time after the patient was dead kind of trying to figure out the forensics themselves but it didn't seem appropriate to do that with the president, but it really wouldn't have mattered because when Earl Rose, who was the new county medical examiner, did his autopsy, if he had questions about the treatment, he would call us. In fact, he frequently called us down just to teach us. He'd call the house staff and say, "OK, here's this patient you treated. Tell me what you did, and let me show you how to recognize exit wounds and entrance wounds, etc." So, we kind of all assumed that there was no reason to roll the president over because Earl Rose would be doing the autopsy. When the president was taken away, we realized, "Gee, the body's gone. Earl's not going to do the autopsy, and these guys aren't going to have any medical records to go by." But that was kind of a medical surprise, if you will. Didn't think about why they would have done that.

Earl Rose was, and I think still is, recognized as one of the really outstanding forensic pathologists in the country. But the reason we're given, and it makes sense . . . is that new President Johnson was not willing to leave Dallas on Air Force One, President Kennedy's plane, without President Kennedy's body.

What I've heard is that President Johnson would not leave without President Kennedy's body, and I don't know any facts. But it makes sense. I mean, he was a pretty shrewd politician, and you can imagine the impact of people saying, "Well, not only did he take the president's job, but he took his plane and left town and left the president in this mess."

. . . the law is, as I understand it, that if you're murdered here, the examination has to be done here. But, gosh, it was the president. There are no laws about shot presidents. And there's no big . . . if

I had been a Secret Service man, I think I'd have done the same thing and had gotten that body out of here and gotten President Johnson out of here because they didn't know if it was a Russian plot . . . they didn't know what was going on. So, their job was to get Johnson to safety.

EARL ROSE, MD

(excerpted from the *Journal of the American Medical Association*, May 1992)

"I was in their way," Rose recalls. "I was face to face with Secret Service Agent Roy H. Kellerman, and I was trying to explain to him that Texas law applied in the instant case of the death of the president and that the law required an autopsy to be performed in Texas.

"Agent Kellerman tried three tactics to have his way—he asserted his identity as representing the Secret Service; he appealed for sympathy to Mrs. Kennedy; and he used body language to attempt to bully, or, should I say, intimidate. I don't recall the exact words, but he and I exchanged firm and emotionally charged words. At no time did I feel I was in physical danger because he and the others were armed. I was not looking at Agent Kellerman's gun, I was looking at his eyes, and they were very intense. His eyes said that he meant to get the president's body back to Washington."

CHAPTER 10

THE GRIEF

My classmate and friend, Cervando Martinez, didn't realize he had been filmed by CBS that day. I spotted his distinctive jaw line at fifty-three seconds into a Dan Rather narrated segment video-taped at the Parkland emergency room loading dock. In it, my friend is clinging to a KEEP RIGHT sign in the driveway of the ER, as though the weight of the moment made it hard to stand.

Most of us stood nearby in an agitated silence of shock and disbelief. This focal point of history unfolding is vividly recalled in nine of the reports that follow. Common threads are the bouquet of bloody roses left in the limousine, the new President Johnson wedged between five Secret Service agents who seemed to carry him to a commandeered car, and a blood-stained Jackie leaving with the bronze casket.

Parkland Hospital Chaplain Kenneth Pepper delivered the sermon at the memorial service held in the staff library at 4:00 p.m., Monday, November 25, 1963. Chaplain Pepper said, "In shocked dismay, we cried out to God at the insult dealt to human dignity by this event."

Jed Rosenthal wrote his mom, ". . . now all the people of these United States are united . . . in a common grief." Stephen Barnett felt, "at a loss to respond, confused between sorrow and rage." This captures very well what gripped our nation, perhaps even more deeply for those who were there when it happened. As Robert Duchouquette begins his narrative poem of those hours, "The whole nation cried the day I met JFK."

Courtesy of the *Dallas Morning News*

Those of us standing around outside the ER saw this wretched sight: The yellow roses of Texas given to Nellie Connally, thrown asunder like our world in those unforgettable hours.

REX COLE, MD

I was told that a classmate, Don Senter, was walking near the entrance to the emergency room when the limousine arrived. He helped get the president on a stretcher.

WILLIAM R. WEAVER, MD

Before entering Southwestern in 1963, I had worked in Washington, D.C. for a California senator in the 87th Congress in 1961. I began work the first week of January 1961 and two weeks later, John F. Kennedy was inaugurated president. Our senator's office had several tickets to the inauguration and the staff drew straws to see who would attend. I was one of the lucky recipients and attended the inauguration on a snowy day, on the east steps of the Capitol, January 20, 1961. Not long after that I sat in the gallery of the House Chamber and witnessed President Kennedy's State of the Union address.

Now, less than three years later, I was a first-year medical student standing in a parking area next to an unoccupied police motorcycle with a hundred or more other people outside the Parkland emergency room awaiting word on the president who had been shot. I had a difficult time putting the memory of the inauguration next to standing outside the Parkland emergency room thinking that the president of the United States was in there and that he had been shot in Dallas and was probably mortally wounded.

We waited a long time and in hindsight, I now know that some of the wait was for the priest to arrive to administer the Last Rites. While waiting, I was hearing the police dispatcher on the motorcycle radio next to me saying they had a suspect in a theater in Oak Cliff.

After the hearse left with the president's body, the crowd dispersed. I made my way back to the medical school via the hospital. Someone alarmingly said while I was walking in the hospital halls that LBJ had been shot, too. I picked up my pace

Courtesy of the Dallas Morning News

Mrs. Dearie Cabell, wife of Dallas Mayor Earle Cabell, riding in a limousine a few cars behind the president, said, "The motorcade stopped dead still when the noise of the shot was heard." Here she sits alone facing the Parkland emergency room loading dock, the last visible member of the presidential entourage.

and made it to the Registrar's office in the school where they were listening to the radio about the assassination. I asked if LBJ had been shot. They said no, there had been no reports of that. The situation was ripe for rumors.

It was a sad day. It seemed that for several days if you went to a restaurant or public place that people were either whispering or talking in low tones in their conversation. I think everyone was in shock.

JOHN BELL, MD

Although some of the memories of the day President Kennedy was killed have faded, others remain keen. . . .

A group of us had completed lunch at the Parkland hospital cafeteria. Because of construction, we had to exit through the emergency room to return to our classroom in the clinical science building where our lectures were held. In retrospect I think I passed through the emergency room as Kennedy was being brought into the emergency room. We had not arrived to the classroom before we heard that Kennedy had been shot and brought to Parkland. We returned through the back side of the clinical science building to watch the emergency room from a distance. Mostly we watched in reverent silence with an occasional soft voice. Rumors abounded, including that both Johnson and Kennedy had been killed. However, the fact that President Kennedy had suffered a probable fatal gunshot wound never changed. Soon news reached us that it had been announced that Kennedy was dead.

Jim Atkins noticed the flag in front of Parkland had not been lowered to half-mast. There was a security guard in front of

Parkland. He said his orders were to keep people from entering the front of Parkland. He did not attempt to prevent us from lowering the flag but he wasn't absolutely sure that President Kennedy was dead. It appeared to me it would have been relatively easy to enter Parkland in the front entrance if one was determined to do so. I went to the classroom and it said on the blackboard something to the effect that classes were cancelled the rest of the day. A number of students and many other people watched the outside of the emergency room in stunned silence for what seemed like hours.

Eventually I and others returned to the fraternity house, Phi Beta Pi. Of course the news was on TV and it provided more accuracy to the events than we had known previously. Details were still unclear, however. This was the only weeknight in the preclinical years that no one made an attempt to study. There was nothing to do but watch TV and it only had the tragic events of the day.

A carload of us decided to go downtown. All businesses including movie theaters and restaurants were closed. The only activity was a man selling a special edition of the newspaper. He was yelling, "Extra, extra, read all about it! Kennedy slain on Dallas streets!"

CHARLES G. BRISENO, MD, AND MARIA ELENA BRISENO

On November 22, 1963, my wife and I had been married less than four months. She was working at a title company in downtown Dallas.

My classmates and I were waiting for a professor to start a class. He was late. We were expecting to be let out of class in a moment's notice, so that we could walk over to the Harry Hines Blvd to watch the John F. Kennedy motorcade drive by the Medical School.

My wife was on her lunch hour and walked a couple of blocks to join a large crowd of people lining the downtown Dallas street and watched President Kennedy and Jackie drive by. She did not hear the shots that rang out a few minutes later but when she returned to her job her coworkers informed her that the president had been shot. Nobody worked at her office after that. She rode the bus home.

At the Medical School, we were suddenly told that the president had been shot. I was shocked. Some students walked over to Parkland. I decided to go home which was at the Projects on Hampton Road at Singleton.

We felt like we had lost a family member. Both of us were sad, anxious, and depressed.

LEWIS RANEY, MD

The day President John Kennedy was assassinated was perhaps the most exciting day and week of my entire career.

There was definitely an atmosphere of concern in Dallas about this new president. Democrats vs. Conservatives.

I was in the E.N.T. Clinic just a few steps away from the emergency room entrance. A door from the waiting room led to the outside sidewalk. I was placing a feeding tube in an elderly lady who had undergone a laryngectomy-cervical pharyngectomy. She was undergoing reconstruction.

We had a small radio in the clinic monitoring the parade event. It was around noon and the announcement was made that the president and governor had been shot. I knew they would be brought to Parkland and I ran out of the above-mentioned door to find the limousine already parked just outside the ER. It wasn't a good sight. I will never forget seeing the flowers in the back seat.

Surrounding the emergency room entrance there was mass chaos. Busses were arriving with the staff and press. I went back to my patient and completed the feeding tube procedure. As I entered the clinic, I heard reporters asking folks to hold this and that telephone and giving them money. We had a bank of public phones just outside the E.N.T. clinic door.

While all of this was happening, I received a phone call from my wife. She was a speech pathologist working in the Hurst-Euless-Bedford Schools. Her principal had rushed to her with the news and asked her to call me. I think that was the last phone call that came in the clinic. Switchboards were taken over by the authorities.

The clinics emptied fast and everyone went home to be glued to their TVs for the next several days. I never did know what happened to so many patients who left without being seen. As well as I remember, I went home also. I do remember going around to an inside entrance to the emergency room and seeing a person guarding that entrance with a gun.

I remember coming back to the hospital to make rounds and the entire hospital grounds (small at the time) were surrounded by police cars—Dallas City, County and State Troopers.

My wife and I, like all others, stayed glued to the TV between calls from all our families wanting more details. My parents called to let me know that Police Officer N.M. "Nick" McDonald had arrested Oswald in the Texas Theater. When we were kids, "Nick"—we called him Maurice—frequently visited his aunt, uncle, and cousins in Paris, Arkansas and we played together.

CERVANDO MARTINEZ, MD

We piled back into the car and drove to Southwestern, parked and rushed to the Parkland ER. We couldn't get in. I spent the next eternity of time outside the ER in the ambulance arrival driveway waiting. Finally a hearse/ambulance arrived and the bronze/gold coffin was wheeled in. We knew what that meant. I don't remember if I waited to see it leave.

SLOAN LEONARD, MD

I was Class of 1965 and was having lunch with my wife—Mary Lois—in the Parkland cafeteria around 11:30 on November 22, seated at a table with a number of classmates. Over the scratchy intercom, there was a page for Shires, Jenkins, Clark, Sanford, etc. to come to the ER. We thought it was unusual but finished our meals. I was on a rotation in the ER as a junior and had my fresh white coat and Littmann stethoscope—and little black book— and went to the elevator to go down to the ER. I got on—it was empty—and when the ground floor door opened, a man in a dark suit with a fedora on stuck a machine gun in my belly and told me to not get off. I assured him I was "Dr. Leonard" and was assigned to the ER. He had no interest in this and forcefully told me to leave. When I got to the first floor (being a twenty-four-year-old ingénue), I raced around Parkland to the ER and saw the doors of the limo hanging open with flowers strewn about. There were a few people around who told me JFK had been shot. A bit later, press started gathering largely black people to stand together and sob so they could capture the "emotion" they felt. At 3:20 p.m.,

I bought on the front steps of Parkland a *Times Herald* special edition I have in front of me now.

"President John F. Kennedy died at 1:00 CST today here in Dallas. He died of a gunshot wound to the brain. I have no details regarding the assassination of the President." This 1:33 p.m. announcement in a Parkland Hospital nurse's classroom by Malcolm Kilduff, the assistant White House Press Secretary, had been delayed by order of the new president, Lyndon Johnson.

LARRY DOSSEY, MD

Classes were dismissed. We students were collectively paralyzed with grief. Four of us drifted aimlessly to a nearby tavern and drank beer in numbed silence. No one could find words to describe adequately what we felt. I still can't.

WILLIAM ZEDLITZ, MD

I met several other residents and nurses coming down the aisles and they asked about the president's status. I told them that it looked like a lethal injury, and the crew was doing all it could to save him but the head injury was so severe that I felt that he had very little chance of survival. At this point, the enormity of the situation began to impress itself upon me. I had been busy up until this time but now I realized the president of the United States was lying in that trauma room with very little chance to make it out alive, and of the momentous consequences of that fact. As I walked back to the elevator I suddenly felt very tired and depressed about the situation, wondering what chain of events would now follow. I remember little else about the rest of the day except sometime later I found myself sitting with my head in my hands with tears running down my cheeks.

CERVANDO MARTINEZ, MD

That evening, several of us Democrats in the class, Byron Howard, David Haymes, Wayne Mathews and our spouses had planned a little party for an old friend of mine from college, John Duncan. John was of course also a Democrat and I think by then Executive Director of the ACLU. He was in town and my friends were eager to meet him. We got together anyhow, but the event turned into a wake. We sat around and cursed the right wing nuts that Dallas was famous for and mourned.

The Board of Managers, Medical Staff and Personnel of the Dallas County Hospital District join the Nation and the World in Mourning the death of President John Fitzgerald Kennedy.

A MEMORIAL

Text of the sermon delivered by Chaplain Kenneth Pepper at the Memorial Service held in the Staff Library at 4:00 p.m., Monday, November 25, 1963.

A crepe hangs solemnly on a surgery room door in the Emergency Department of our hospital which speaks symbolically of the events of the past few days. It speaks of an event for which we are all grievously shamed and sorrowful. It speaks for our feelings which have been bruised and grieved by the personal loss of our President. It represents the fact that each of us played a part in this world drama which happened in our hometown and even within the walls of the hospital itself. It thus becomes fitting that we should join hands with our nation in mourning to view the events of recent days and to pay solemn honor to the man who has shouldered the leadership of government in this all too short space of time.

John Fitzgerald Kennedy, young in body, vigorous in mind, dedicated in spirit, has been taken from us. Over the din of a multitude of cheering voices rang out three shots which cut down our president and seriously wounded our governor. Neither the skill nor wisdom of the medical team, nor the resources of the richest nation on the Earth, nor the hopes and daydreams nourished in our breasts nor the earnest prayers of our souls was able to hold back the reality that the assassin's bullet had found its mark! In shocked dismay we cried out to God at the insult dealt to human dignity by this event.

Today we mourn his passing. We remember his concern for civil liberties and his concern for the underprivileged. We remember his faith in education and training and ultimate concern for the sick and the aged. Many have watched his work and have seen in him the work of an emancipator. Many of us were critical of his methods or ideas but all of us have been sharpened by the encounter with his life and leadership. We remember his family and in prayer hold them up to God that His grace may abound. In this memorial we honor the memory of our President taken in violent death.

Patrolman J. D. Tippitt, strong in heart, faithful and dedicated in service was also taken from us. Relatively unknown to us personally, yet symbolically representative of all of those who stand as a shield against evil, he gave his life in the exercise of his duty. We mourn his passing today. We memorialize his life and hold his family in prayer in these moments of worship.

Parkland is a hospital where the struggle between life and death, disease and health is our bread and meat. Rarely a 24 hour period passes that doesn't bring to our doors someone with a story of tragedy, suffering, injustice or violence. To each of these we offer an outstretched hand – sometimes to cure often to relieve and always to comfort.

The events of the last few days have reached us all. The President, the Governor and even their possible assassin have invaded our lives in a very personal way. Although the hospi-

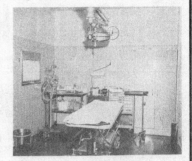

Floral Spray placed on the door of Trauma Room No. 1 during the funeral services of President Kennedy

At 9:00 a.m., Monday, November 25, 1963, at the hour funeral ceremonies got underway in Washington, D. C., for President John F. Kennedy, a floral spray was placed on the door of Trauma Room No. 1 in Parkland's Emergency Room.

The spray marked the spot where less than three days earlier the President died after being struck by the bullets of an assassin.

Members of the administrative staff placed the spray of white carnations on the door in the name of the Board of Managers, Medical Staff and all personnel of the Dallas County Hospital District.

Chaplain Kenneth Pepper led the group in prayer as Emergency Room personnel and patients looked on.

During the time of the funeral, and ever since the death of the President, Trauma Room No. 1, has been used only when absolutely necessary.

A number of suggestions have been made for memorializing the room where the President died, but no definite plans have been announced by the Board of Managers.

tal personnel performed as a highly skilled team we experienced the shock and the deep hurt of an intense grief feeling. The traumatic invasion of evil and destruction is not new to us but the scope of these events have left our feelings bruised and grieving.

We are not alone in our grief. Our city and our state stands under the shadow of this event with the sick feelings of a World community ready to erupt in the scape-goatings of their vengeance. Dallas and the State of Texas bear a scar which will not heal quickly and which will be long remembered. As citizens we feel a hurt and shame which only God can heal. The blackness of the hour hangs heavily over us.

Death is always a cruel irreversible reality. We wrestle and struggle with the grim reaper but our success only buys for us a little more time. But for God in His eternity, we would all be lost! Neither shame, nor guilt nor death will conquer us in God.

"Death is swallowed up in victory. O death, where is thy victory? O death, where is thy sting? The sting of death is sin; and the power of sin is the law: But thanks be to God, who giveth us the victory through our Lord Jesus Christ." (1 Corinthians 15:54-57.)

Hope is not lost, even in our own hospital our Governor has experienced a physical victory over this evil. Our Country's leadership has rallied to the crisis and brought unity out of the chaos. The pages of our quest of liberty is writ largely with the blood stains of patriots – both of the great and of the unknown.

Dallas bears its scar but even this can stimulate its greatness. Dallas will lift its head in forgiveness and honor. Texas will move in its tradition of undaunted bigness and integrity. In the God who is the giver of life and honor we shall have victory and life.

Trauma Room No. 1

STEPHEN BARNETT, MD

I remember feeling stunned—at a loss to respond, confused between sorrow and rage, but left in an empty hole the rest of the afternoon.

Robert Duchouquette, MD

As the country mourned, I too was caught up in the grief of the nation and the appalling historic sight I had witnessed.

Courtesy of the Dallas Morning News

This was the last scene we would see that terrible day: the white hearse nearly under the wing of Air Force One.

CHAPTER 11

DALLAS

The night before the assassination, my classmate David Haymes and others gathered in the north-facing pathology room to review microscopic slides before the next day's exam. A screech of tires drew them to the windows where they saw a shower of papers flutter to the ground and the fast receding taillights of the car from which they had been thrown. When they saw the hundreds of variously colored leaflets, all with front and side views of President Kennedy, and boldly proclaiming WANTED FOR TREASON, they called the police.

Also on this day before, Raoul Berke has never forgotten a classmate saying, "You know, somebody ought to shoot that sumbitch." And Al Lindsey recalls his minister's sermon the Sunday after the president died calling on Dallas to acknowledge it was a "city full of hatred, a perfect environment for such an event to take place." Yet, there was not a single hostile demonstration from the people of Dallas. Cervando Martinez saw to it that the second story of his parents' house on the motorcade's route from the airport was prominently draped in a sheet painted with an exuberant red: "VIVA KENNEDY!"

Leslie Moore recalls during his later internship interviews, ". . . everywhere, and I mean everywhere, I went, people cursed Dallas."

Wayne Smith remembers a TV anchor from a Washington DC station commenting on the hatred "everyone in Texas had for President Kennedy and particularly anyone residing in Dallas."

Courtesy of David Haymes, MD

Of course this was, and shall forever remain, wholly irrational and based entirely on the human mind's unfortunate tendency to need—and even create—a bad guy. Pain and anger do strange things to the human psyche . . . but to blame a city of 700,000? Nobody seems to blame (or even credit!) Dallas for killing Oswald. And Jack Ruby blamed "temporal lobe epilepsy."

DAVID HAYMES, MD

November 21 was a beautiful clear day in the low seventies and a waxing crescent moon appeared as darkness descended over the fledgling UTSMS campus and Parkland Hospital. Several sophomore medical students had gathered in the north-facing pathology room that evening to review microscope slides when our concentration was broken by the shrieking of tires on pavement. We raced to the window to see only receding tail lights and a shower of papers fluttering to the ground. We raced down stairs and discovered hundreds of leaflets on pink and green and orange paper all saying—WANTED FOR TREASON—accompanied by a frontal and side mug shot of our President. We gathered up as many as we could and called the police. "No, we didn't see who did it" and "Yes, this is all of them." But of course it wasn't. One is on display at the Sixth Floor Museum and I have had one of each color all these years.

CERVANDO MARTINEZ, MD

On that fateful November day I was a sophomore in medical school back in my hometown for my medical education. Kennedy's route was known because the evening before I went to my parent's home at 2537 Cedar Springs to prepare a sign welcoming JFK. My parents liked him and of course Cedar Springs Road is the main avenue from Love Field to downtown Dallas. We were sure that the motorcade would pass by the house and so we took an old bed sheet and wrote, "VIVA KENNEDY" on it. Then we climbed out a second story window and tacked it on the wall of the second floor. My brother Rene, who was in high school then, helped me.

PETER WILES, MD

Do not forget those were angry times in Dallas. Shortly before the assassination, a bullet was fired into the Turtle Creek home of Major General Walker and Adlai Stevenson's talk (which I attended) was marred by picketing and a demonstration during which he was spat upon and struck with a picket sign! Based on his experience and evaluation, he advised JFK to cancel his Dallas trip, but Lyndon persuaded him to go.

RAOUL BERKE, MD

In November 1963, I was doing my Junior Medicine rotation at the VA. At breakfast, one of my classmates said, "You know, somebody ought to shoot that sumbitch, Kennedy." There was general agreement among his buddies, all members of the same fraternity. At lunch, sitting with the same group, the same classmate said, "Well, they shouldn't have shot him—he's a father." That evening, I sought tearful solace with one of the few other liberal, pro-Kennedy students in our class, and her college-professor husband. I remember this vividly, word-for-word. I left Dallas after graduation; I have never returned.

H. Wayne Smith, MD

I recall one TV anchor representing Washington, DC commenting on the hatred everyone in Texas had for President Kennedy and in particular anyone residing in Dallas.

It was a sad day indeed—even the next year when I was a Fellow in Infectious Disease at University of Colorado in Denver, I was treated with distaste for several weeks because I was at Parkland that day.

Leslie Moore, MD

In the weeks following the assassination, I was in the Northeast and Midwest, interviewing for internships and everywhere, and I mean everywhere I went, people cursed Dallas.

Al Lindsey, MD

The other really memorable occurrence was the sermon that Reverend Bill Holmes preached at Northaven Methodist Church that Sunday morning. He described the full-page black-bordered announcement in the *Dallas Morning News* that said of JFK "this man is a traitor!" Then he told us of the fifth (I think) grade classroom in Dallas in which the teacher rushed in tears sobbing "the President's been shot," and the children cheered. His sermon title was "One Thing Worse Than This," and his point was that the one thing worse than the assassination would be for Dallas not to acknowledge that it was a city full of hatred, a perfect environment for such an event to take place. My sense of Dallas has never been less than *very* ambivalent since that day.

RON JONES, MD

(oral history courtesy of the Sixth Floor Museum)

I thought Dallas was a progressive community. I think that was about the era when Erik Jonsson was mayor, and he had set out to establish some goals for Dallas, some long-range goals. So, it was a progressive city. There were a lot of major sport activities available in Dallas and the symphony and the opera and all the things that you would like to have available to you whether you'd utilize them or not [smiling] when you live in a large city. But I think that what I noticed most was that it was a progressive city. We thought that the schools were good [nodding] in Dallas at that time.

As I recall, it was fairly quick. There was reaction to this. I . . . you sensed that even President Kennedy's family may have had some resentment toward Dallas because, you know, this was a tragedy that had occurred. It could've occurred anywhere, but unfortunately, it occurred in Dallas. And so, I think Dallas caught the brunt of that. Here was a city that thought like that when, in fact, probably no one from Dallas even had anything to do with this."

JAMES CARRICO, MD

(oral history courtesy of the Sixth Floor Museum)

Some of my colleagues have some stories. Some of them were somewhat cynical. One of our residents, Bill Stone, who's now in practice in Hobbs, New Mexico, was, I believe, in Korea shortly after that. . . . Apparently, the story goes, Bill was in Korea and there was still a lot of ugly talk and giving people a bad time about the president dying, etc. And Bill was really kind of a character, either quieted things down or made it worse by saying, "Well, you know, we could have saved him if we wanted to." But that was maybe . . . not obviously appropriate and obviously not true, but it was hard to just keep your cool. I think one of the things I learned from that whole business is how important it is to keep your cool and be moderate and careful in your statements. I mean, if you're . . . I think it's fair to say that all the stuff in the paper, all the real extremism that existed in Dallas right then, did two things. Well, it may have made a guy like Oswald think that doing something like assassinating the president would have been accepted. I mean, if you're kind of a nut and you're reading in the paper, "Go home. We don't want you." Or hearing people say, "This guy ought to be shot." A nut could do that. The other thing it did clearly is once the president was shot here, all that was remembered and clearly we bought some of our own negative representation by what we had said ahead of time. So, I guess a take-home which I believe, I guess I've always believed it, but I believe even more is that extreme statements are liable to get you in trouble.

The only difficulty at all . . . the Warren Commission gave none. The only criticisms of how Kennedy was treated came from two very different sources. In one of those letters I talked about they said, you know, "You guys let the president die." And that was obviously nuts. And then the press made a big deal about not turning the president over and looking at his back. As a matter of fact, I was called one night at home a couple of days after the assassination by a reporter, trying to ask me why . . . why we hadn't seen those wounds in the back. And I kind of explained it . . . or tried to explain it like I did to you guys. The headlines the next day were "Dallas doctors fail to look at president's back." That's when I learned the value of "no comment." My respect for reporters didn't go up dramatically during those couple of years.

ROBERT MCCLELLAND, MD

(oral history courtesy of the Sixth Floor Museum)

And you sort of got the idea that probably the great majority of people in Dallas didn't care much one way or the other. They were traditional Southern Democrats if you happened to ask them about it, but that wasn't really anybody's interest. They were just mostly making their way, and that was it. And I think as more and more . . . as the Cold War got colder or hotter, however you want to look at it, and people got worried about it. I can remember when we were storing things in the basement of Parkland. We had a, you know, a person at the medical school, Dr. Sanford, who's now dead, who was charged with setting up shelters, you know, for when the bomb hit us, and that there was water and food and things like that stored in Parkland where we would . . . was one of the places that we would go. So, there was a rising awareness of this and an increasing suspicion.

Right after I got here in '57, and I remember walking around in the basement, the sub-basement of Parkland and seeing those large canisters of water and whatnot stored there. And I remember particularly after, you know, the Bay of Pigs and the missile crisis things that there were a lot them in. . . . Especially the missile crisis. I was living over in East Dallas in that time. I was a resident, and we were all talking about digging holes in the ground at that time, so there was an increasing paranoia and fearfulness here in the early '60s.

Stevenson was here, and he had been hit in the head with a sign [chuckling]. Whether it was purposeful or accidental, I expect it may have been a little bit of purpose behind it . . . by some lady, I think, who lived in Highland Park, and quite a bit was made of that both at the time and then particularly shortly after that when the assassination occurred . . . that this was brought up again that this was the city of hate and all of these terrible right-wing people here and so on. And they set up sort of . . . set Dallas up as the ideal place for this to . . . where you'd expect something like this to happen, you know. Of course, many Dallasites, I think, you'd have to agree that there was an element of that here, but to take that brush and tar the whole city with it always struck me as being rather unfair. Understandable perhaps that some people might want to do that and would tend to do that, but still, you know, not saying that the whole city is a city of hate and everybody in it is bad, particularly a large city like that . . . not too good.

CHAPTER 12

OSWALD AND RUBY

The Dallas City Jail employed Southwestern's medical students, interested in the hands-on experience but mostly eager for the money, to see to the medical needs of the prisoners. Even freshmen were "jail doctors." Now, this was not only practicing medicine without benefit of licensure, but also practicing medicine without benefit of *knowing anything*!

My friend, Bill Hall (oh, so missed) worked at the jail the evening of the assassination and showed me a copy of the police report, the title of which read, "Name: John Fitzgerald Kennedy. Occupation: President of the United States."

Another classmate, David Haymes, had traded his shift that Sunday morning to senior medical student, Fred Bieberdorf, so missed being responsible for Oswald's care. The story I was told is that when Oswald was shot, nobody could find the keys for the jail's emergency medical supply cabinets. Considering the nature of his injuries, it is unlikely that anything done at the jail would have altered the outcome.

The sheriff in the white suit who was walking next to Oswald when Ruby shot him, bent over close to the prostrate prisoner and said, "You're hurt pretty bad, son. Is there anything you want to say?" Oswald slowly shook his head, closed his eyes and said nothing.

On duty in the Psychiatry ER was senior Harry Eastman who saw the Secret Service, machine guns drawn, seal the ER and "a person was whisked by on a gurney, through the ER to the elevators to the surgery floor." Kenneth Farrimond was told there was, "an FBI agent with a badge and a gun in the room ready to take a deathbed confession if Oswald were to survive."

Wayne Delaney had just finished a pediatric surgery case when Oswald was brought to the operating room. Remarkably, he saw surgery begin less than ten minutes after Oswald arrived at the ER. He watched the chief of surgery, Tom Shires, and Doctors McClelland, Perry and Jones control the bleeding from the aorta, renal artery, and vena cava, while pumping sixteen pints of blood into Oswald.

Then his heart arrested, and even open chest cardiac massage could not save him. His death left us with a question we shall never hear answered: Who killed our JFK?

HARRY EASTMAN, MD

Sunday I was on duty in the psych ER and suddenly all the doors were sealed with some men in suits with machine guns drawn. A person was whisked on a gurney through the ER to the elevators to the surgery floor. It was stated that it was Lee Harvey Oswald. The ER was sealed for a period of time and I remember looking at the people lined up who otherwise would have been patients.

Later, perhaps after a couple of years, I was a medicine resident on infectious disease when Jack Ruby was hospitalized

Courtesy of Bob Jackson

Twenty million viewers recoiled at the first televised assassination. It didn't seem to matter that Oswald was the most hated man in the world at that moment. Photographer Bob Jackson caught this historic moment for which he was awarded the Pulitzer Prize. For many, this was the most shocking image of those tragic forty-eight hours.

with pneumonia. I remember his sister sitting outside his room daily, asking me for information as we made rounds; a very plain appearing woman, opposite the image of a flamboyant Jack Ruby in his heyday.

RONALD O. WYATT, MD

I had a job at night at the Dallas County jail. Saturday night before Oswald was to be transferred from the city jail to the county jail, I was told I would have to stay at the jail until the transfer had been completed. About mid-Sunday a.m., a number of sirens went by the county jail. It wasn't too long the warden called me and said I could go home. Oswald had been shot and was taken to Parkland Hospital.

One other event occurred to me related to the Kennedy shooting. One evening the warden called and said Jack Ruby was injured and needed a doctor. A group of guards came and took me to the floor Ruby was being held. After going through four to five sliding doors plus multiple guards, I finally arrived at Ruby's cell. He was a very pleasant person. I asked what type of medical symptoms he was having; he told me he had slipped out of his bed and scraped his head. I examined the scrape and gave him a tube of antibiotic ointment. Interestingly his cell was filled with cards and letters. He told me people were sending him money and gifts. They were glad he had killed Oswald.

DAVID HAYMES, MD

Two days later on Sunday I was to have worked as the "jail doctor" at the Dallas city jail. But for reasons long forgotten I switched with Fred Bieberdorf. The "jail doctor" was a medical student who stayed in the parking basement. So Fred was there when Jack Ruby shot Lee Harvey Oswald. There but for the grace of God. . . .

On January 3, 1967 as an intern I was on the sixth floor of Parkland when Jack Ruby died, just down the hall from where I was making rounds. He had been defended by Melvin Belli but also by a local attorney, Phil Burleson. I went to high school with Phil's sister-in-law, and Phil was my patient until he died in 1995.

LEWIS RANEY, MD

On Sunday, November 24, we were driving from Irving, Texas on the Stemmons Freeway and there was an announcement that Lee Harvey Oswald had been shot and was being taken to Parkland. I only remember the excitement of people running, grouping, talking, etc. I made hospital rounds on my patients and left. The operating room doors were guarded. I didn't even consider going on the floor where Governor Connally was located.

KENNETH FARRIMOND, MD

That Sunday morning we were in the anatomy lab studying for Monday's practical when someone came to tell us that Oswald had been shot. He was in the OR at Parkland with an FBI agent with a badge and a gun in the room, ready to take a deathbed statement if Oswald were to survive.

KEN WALLACE, MD

He (Carrico) also told about the Sunday when Oswald was taken to surgery. They opened him up and he had an abdomen full of blood. He had a tear in the vena cava, renal vein and hepatic vein, as I recall. They controlled the bleeding, replaced fluids and thought they could close and he would make it, when he fibrillated. After forty-five minutes of trying to defib, they quit. Carrico said that Oswald almost survived that gunshot wound. Think what a historical difference that would have made.

WAYNE DELANEY, MD

I had just finished doing a case on a pediatric patient when Oswald was brought to the ER. It was my understanding that only ten minutes elapsed from the time he was brought in until he was in the operating room on the second floor.

I watched his operation performed by Dr. Tom Shires, the chief of surgery. I could be wrong, but it seems like he was assisted by Dr. Kemp Clark, who was chief of neurosurgery. There were at least two other people scrubbed in, but I don't remember who they were. I just remember that single bullet hitting the vena cava, aorta and renal artery among a host of other things. They were doing cardiac massage and sewing leads to the heart before it was all over.

RON JONES, MD

(oral history courtesy of the Sixth Floor Museum)

But Sunday morning, I had . . . we didn't have much time off, and it happened early Sunday morning. There was a barbershop at the bowling alley at Inwood and Lemmon [smiling], and you could . . . they were open on Sunday morning.

And you needed a haircut once in a while [smiling], and so I thought I would run over and get a haircut quickly on Sunday morning. It's a quiet time. And we didn't have beepers, and so everybody . . . you had to let everybody know where you were. And I got a call that there had been a stab wound to the neck come into the emergency room, and I was on-call with the residents that day. And so, I left the barbershop to go over to be present for that surgery. And I was waiting outside in the operating room lounge while the residents were finishing up with this relatively minor stab wound to the neck, and the telephone rang. And the nurse answered, and after a short time, turned to me and she said, "They've shot Oswald, and they're bringing him to the emergency room."

And that again was a pretty significant impact having just gone through this trauma for the weekend up until that, having Connally in the hospital and all the security that was around. There was security in the operating room on all the floors. Connally's rooms were heavily secured. And here we had to deal with another episode. Again, that was not a great deal of surprise because it had been pretty well publicized, as I recall, in the newspapers and TV when Oswald was to be moved and how he was to be moved, where he was to be moved, the time that he was going to be moved.

And so, that was pretty well known. I walked out in the hall, and as I was going down the hall, the office door to Dr. Jenkins's office was open and he was in there—the chairman of anesthesia—and across the desk was Dr. Perry. So here the three of us were again in the same situation we had been in on Friday morning. And I went in and told them that Oswald had been shot and that they were bringing him to the emergency room.

I thought we would call Dr. Tom Shires who was chairman of the department of surgery at that time, and so I made a phone call to his home. And Mrs. Shires answered and said, "He's not here." And so, I hung up, called again because I thought maybe he was there but on Sunday morning he wasn't answering, and I said, "They've shot Oswald is the reason I was calling, and I just wondered if he could come out." And she said, "I really had seen that before you called the first time [smiling] and knew why you were calling, but he really isn't here."

So, Dr. Jenkins and Dr. Perry and I went to the emergency room, and we got to the emergency room before Oswald arrived—just shortly before. He was wheeled in on a cart, and because there had been all the questions of whether the president was alive or not when he came to the emergency room, I listened to the heart. Lee Harvey Oswald was alive when he came into the emergency room. He was not moving. He had shallow respirations, but he had a heartbeat. And so, we immediately started resuscitation.

And Dr. Jenkins put an endotracheal tube in to get an airway. And it so happened [smiling and shaking head] that I could see the vein in his arm in the same place that I saw one on Kennedy. And so, I did a cutdown on the arm and put in a catheter. And looking at his injuries, he had been shot one time just above the ribcage in the . . . what appeared to be probably the left chest perhaps. Not knowing for sure whether it had entered the chest, decided to put a chest tube in place. Put a tube in the chest. Made a small incision the same way on the left side as we had with Kennedy and put that tube in. And within about six or seven minutes from the time that he came into the emergency room, we had the IV going, the endotracheal tube in, the chest tube in, and we were on our way up the elevator to the operating room [nodding].

And at that time, we had an elevator that was designed to go directly from the emergency room to the second floor and open directly into the operating room. However, you could get access to that elevator on the first floor. And as I recall, either Mr. Fritz or Curry was on that elevator as we took Oswald up, and the elevator stopped not on the second floor but on that first floor. And as the doors opened, news people were there and cameras were flashing, getting . . . trying to get pictures of Oswald on that stretcher. And that really perturbed the police that were on the elevator, and as I recall, whoever was on there with us said, "I'm going to get off and arrest those people." And then he realized, "No, I have to stay with Oswald and get him to the operating room." But that really frustrated the police that there was that intervention and time delay of a minute maybe at that point.

We went on into the operating suite, and Dr. Shires had actually been going home, heard it on the radio—he had been to Parkland earlier that morning—turned around, and was in the emergency room before we took Oswald up to the OR. So, Dr. Shires was the surgeon, Dr. Perry was first assistant, Dr. Robert McClelland was second assistant, and I was the third assistant. So, the four of us operated on Oswald.

It took, as I recall, close to an hour before we finally . . . before he finally died. We did not have any blood pressure palpable or measurable when we got him to the operating room. Dr. Jenkins was the anesthesiologist and I don't believe gave any anesthetic but just gave oxygen. And we . . . an incision was made in the midline, and his abdomen was opened. And there was a tremendous amount of blood in the abdomen [shaking head], and his injuries had been from the . . . where the missile entered, it had gone through the lower part of his left chest and through the diaphragm and the spleen, and as I recall, had gone behind the abdominal cavity in an area that we call the retro peritoneum. And then the retro peritoneum, behind the stomach area is where your aorta is, which is the main artery from the heart, and the inferior vena cava, which brings back all the blood from the lower part of the body to the heart. And he had blown apart the . . . a major vessel off of the aorta, which is the superior mesenteric artery, which supplies the intestine with its blood supply—a large, major vessel. Plus, now the aorta is now open, and every time the heart beats, you get a tremendous amount of blood loss. He had also gone through that inferior vena cava, the major vein, and on into the right kidney and probably the pancreas and had injured the right renal artery and vein. So, he had a tremendous amount of blood vessel damage, and as exposure was obtained and the vessels were identified and were occluded—were clamped—that took, you know, thirty minutes or so, and he . . . I think Dr. Jenkins had told us that his pressure eventually got up to about 60 millimeters of mercury, which is only about half [smiling] what a normal person's blood pressure would be.

So, he really never showed any signs of rapid recovery to say the least, but we did get control of this massive bleeding. But, about the time we got control, his blood pressure dropped again, and then he died. We opened the left chest, and the chest tube was in place. And we did some open cardiac massage, but we were never able to resuscitate him, and he died shortly after 1:00 p.m. that day [nodding].

Again, several people did come into the operating room and were in the hall outside the operating room. I do recall one of the radiology residents, as I recall, trying to take pictures during the operation, and his camera and film [smiling] was confiscated very quickly by the police. And I'm not sure [smiling] he ever saw those pictures, or even got his camera back. But there was fairly tight security going on at that time because we still had Governor Connally in the hospital and not far away on that same floor [nodding].

My thinking at that time was that he probably was the assassin, but I had to go on was what everybody else had to go on and that was the television and news media. And I thought very likely that he was probably the one that had shot the president, and I think that's the way we approached him. But by the same token, it didn't influence what we did.

But in one sense, it's a little ironic that you go through resuscitation of somebody [smiling], knowing that if they are guilty, that they're probably going to get a death sentence, too. But you would've liked to have saved Oswald because he might've been able to furnish you with a tremendous amount of information [smiling]. And it might or might not have made any difference in the outcome of how this evolved and what was behind the assassination. But for over and above the fact that you wanted to save a life on an individual, you always wanted to save it for that reason as well.

ROBERT McCLELLAND, MD

(oral history courtesy of the Sixth Floor Museum)

Sunday morning, of course, I was . . . we were getting up and were going to lunch with my mother who was visiting there, and my children . . . my two children and my wife, and as I said, I didn't have the TV on. I was downstairs in the living room waiting for them and so, just to kill time, I leaned over and turned the TV on. And as the screen was, you know, filling up with the picture, I could hear the sound first. And they were saying, "He's been shot! He's been shot!" And then the picture came on, and I saw all this scuffling, you know, going around. And then it became clear very quickly who they were talking about. And I thought, "Well, my goodness. What next?" [chuckling] You know, and so I walked over to the foot of the stairs and yelled up to my wife and told her, I said, "You all will have to go to lunch without me. I've got to go back to Parkland." I said, "They've shot Oswald."

And so, I got in my car and drove back out there, and as I was driving toward Parkland on Beverly, I'd just gotten past Preston and was driving down Beverly, I saw Dr. Shire's car. I recognized it coming toward me, toward his house. He had been to Parkland, and so I guess he had had his radio on. But anyway, he flashed his lights at me and stopped, and I stopped, and so we exchanged information with one another about what he had just heard and what I had just seen. So, he turned around and followed me, and we both got out to Parkland about the same time, and we drove out pretty quickly, of course. And we got there, and I remember walking in the . . . we pulled up and parked right behind the emergency room, which we could do at that time, and ran in there, and they had just gotten there with Oswald, and everybody was still pretty much on tenterhooks from what all had been going on the last two days, and the residents there in the emergency room had gotten, you know, a call that they were bringing him in.

So, they very quickly . . . probably more quickly than had ever been done before or since, got an inter-tracheal tube into him, did cutdowns, as I recall, on him, began to pump uncrossed matched blood into him because he looked like, when I walked into the room and they were doing all this, he was bled out and looked like he was just about gone himself. But they got him pumped back up and got him upstairs, and we had his abdomen open. I think someone who had looked at the time said it was around thirty minutes from the time he was shot, we had his abdomen open in the operating room and were exploring him, and Dr. Shires was the surgeon and Dr. Perry and I were helping him, and he got a clamp on his aorta and venacava right up underneath the diaphragm and got the bleeding stopped because he had been shot through both the aorta and venacava which is a . . . he really probably wouldn't normally have even made it up to the operating room had it not been under the circumstances that it was, and then after that, we were able to be able to expose . . . try to expose the wounds after he had gotten a clamp on up above them. And we worked on him for a good while. I can't remember exactly, but then he arrested, and we first tried closed-chest massage, which they really had only started doing that not too long before that. There had been some papers written about it, and that didn't seem to be working, and so we opened his chest and Dr. Perry and I took turns massaging his heart and finally it just got flabbier and flabbier, and we couldn't get any activity. So, he was declared dead.

ROBERT McCLELLAND, MD

(excerpted from *D Magazine*, October 28, 2008)

When Kennedy arrived, every faculty member on site was called into the emergency room. With Oswald, there were only a few doctors working on him. Twenty-eight minutes after Jack Ruby's shot, they were inside Oswald's abdomen. "He was as white as this piece of paper," McClelland tells the med students. "He had lost so much blood. If he hadn't turned when he saw Ruby coming, he might have been all right." When Oswald saw the gun in Ruby's hand, he had cringed slightly, flinching. Because of this, the bullets went through his aorta and inferior vena cava, the two main blood vessels in the back of the abdominal cavity. There was enormous loss of blood. The medical team pumped pint after pint of untyped blood, sixteen in all, through his body. Shires and Perry eventually got a vascular clamp to stop the bleeding, and the two set about clearing away intestines to get enough room to repair the damage.

They worked on Oswald for an hour when his heart arrested. The blood loss was just too much, and the brief but severe shock too damaging. Perry opened Oswald's chest, and he and McClelland, who was also assisting, took turns administering an open heart massage.

"You pumped Oswald's heart in your hands?" a student asks.

"We took turns, each going until we got tired. We went for, oh, about forty minutes."

The heart got flabbier and flabbier. They squeezed and pumped. The blood around his heart collected on their gloves. Then, no more. Almost two hours after being shot, Lee Harvey Oswald was pronounced dead. The first live homicide on public television was witnessed by twenty million viewers.

The entire emergency room was in a daze. First, the president. Two days later, in the room next door, the president's assassin. It was as if the community had tumbled into one of Rod Serling's *Twilight Zone* episodes.

CHAPTER 13

THE NECK WOUND AND THE CONSPIRACIES

Lyndon Johnson's first executive order as president was issued in the Parkland emergency room and was a conspiracy of sorts, albeit brief and in the interest of national security. The Associated Press reported that LBJ was waiting in a room adjacent to Trauma Room 1 when White House Press Secretary Malcolm Kilduff simply walked up to Johnson and addressed him as "Mr. President." Ladybird let out a short scream as the news hit. Jack Bell's 1965 book reports that President Johnson then told Secretary Kilduff, "I think I had better get out of here . . . before you announce it. We don't know whether this is a worldwide conspiracy, whether they are after me as they were President Kennedy. . . ." The press secretary was then ordered to delay the announcement of JFK's death until the new president was safely aboard Air Force One.

A Secret Service agent assigned to protect the First Lady was riding on the running board of the "back up" limousine ten feet behind the president when he was shot. After nearly five decades, the surviving agents who were in the motorcade that day have revealed what they saw, heard, and felt in those terrible moments. Clint Hill was the agent clinging to the trunk of the presidential limousine in the Zapruder film. He guided Jackie back into her seat and shielded her and the dying president with his body until they reached Parkland Hospital. Hill is quoted in *The Kennedy Detail*: "I heard the first shot, saw the president grab his throat, lurch to the left. . . ."

Though accepting that a second shot, which blew out the back of the President's head, came from above and to the right (the book depository), many conspiracy theorists will not let go of the neck wound as evidence of a second shooter.

Years after the Warren Commission Report, the House Select Committee on Assassinations issued its final report in March 1979, concluding that President John F. Kennedy was probably assassinated "as a result of a conspiracy." They didn't, however, say which one. Based on "various scientific projects," the House Committee suspected there were two gunmen. In *JFK: Breaking the Silence,* author Bill Sloan mentions the eyewitness account of the deaf-mute man, Ed Hoffman, who saw the motorcade from an overpass. Hoffman reports he had a clear view of the grassy knoll and his attention was arrested by the puff of white smoke from a rifle, fired by a man in a suit from behind the white fence. The police, overwhelmingly busy and without an interpreter, apparently never focused on what he had to say.

Moreover, as was described in the highly scientific 2010 book *Head Shot* by G. Paul Chambers, the paraffin test of Oswald's cheek showed *no nitrates*, a near impossibility if Oswald had recently fired a rifle. Though there seems little doubt Oswald killed Officer Tippit with a handgun, and thus the positive nitrate test of his hands, the negative findings on his face hang unexplained in the corridors of time.

The conspiracy theories had something for everyone, as mentioned in a recent *New York Times* article: "Leftists could blame the CIA; the right wingers could blame the communists." There were those who blamed the mafia, or the Cubans—though one had a choice here between the members of the Cuban government who were seeking revenge for CIA assassination plots against Castro, versus the right wing expatriates who believed Kennedy had done too little to overthrow communism on their island. It had been a year since the abortive Bay of Pigs invasion.

Conspiracy theories have been fueled by questions regarding the autopsy done on the president. No autopsy was done in Dallas. Dr. Earl Rose's unsuccessful standoff with the Secret Service led to the autopsy being done at the Bethesda Naval Hospital. One doctor alleged that the tracheotomy incision was deliberately altered before the official autopsy photos were taken. Others present in Trauma Room 1 who reviewed those photos disagreed. Although Dr. Rose thought the Bethesda Naval Hospital autopsy was "less than optimal," he warned, "Do not attribute to conspiracy what can be explained by distrust, inexperience, or ineptitude."

However, the fact remains that the Parkland surgeons were the only physicians to see the neck wound *before* the tracheotomy. Four of the attending surgeons, Kemp Clark, Charles Crenshaw, Robert McClelland, and Malcolm Perry, each an expert in the treatment of gunshot wounds believed at the time that the neck wound was an entry wound.

There is also a problem with the *type* of autopsy performed at Bethesda Naval Hospital. It was undertaken at the request of Mrs. Kennedy and was *not* a forensic autopsy, as would have been performed by Dr. Rose at Parkland.

Dr. McClelland and Dr. Ron Jones are the last survivors among the surgeons who struggled in vain to save the president.

Dr. McClelland continues to believe what he told *D Magazine* in October 2008, that JFK was shot first from the front. That's what he saw in the Zapruder film, the "lurch back and to the left," just as Secret Service agent Clint Hill, revealed after nearly fifty years of silence in *The Kennedy Detail.*

However, when I spoke recently to Dr. Jones, who is chief of surgery at Baylor Hospital, he told me he now believes the neck wound could well have been the result of a bone fragment of the exploding skull (at the time he told the Warren Commission he believed it to be an entry wound). He also points out the weakness in the front shot theory, this being the fact that there was no bullet track from the neck to the posterior skull. Jones was kind enough to send me his recollections as they appeared in the publication *Baylor Reflections.*

Sixteen forensic pathologists had examined the evidence and *all* of them concluded the bullet that killed the president came from behind and above the motorcade. However, none of them had actually examined the body of the dead president.

When the whole of the Kennedy assassination papers are released in 2017, there may be answers to some of these questions. One we would like explained is why the Justice Department continues to refuse to honor a Congressional resolution demanding an end to the secrecy surrounding the death of JFK. As Earl Rose observed in 1992 in the *Journal of the American Medical Association,* "Silence and concealment are the mother's milk of conspiracy theories."

RON JONES, MD

(oral history courtesy of the Sixth Floor Museum)

As I looked at the president, what I saw in just a few seconds was what I thought was a very small entrance wound in the midline of the neck just above the notch in the neck. And it never occurred to me that that was anything but an entrance wound at that time. [pointing to center of neck just above shirt collar] There was enough open here that I could see the wound, and it, as I recall, was just above the collar. I think subsequent photographs show that there perhaps was a nick in the top of the tie in the collar of the shirt. But I could see the wound the way it was . . . the way the president was positioned when I walked in the room. And I thought that it was about a quarter of an inch in diameter, relatively smooth edges. And my interpretation was, he's been shot from the front. That's all I saw at that time, and I knew there was some injury to the head because there was a lot of blood around.

ROBERT McCLELLAND, MD

(excerpted from *D Magazine*, October 28, 2008)

As their fingers moved in and out of the president's body, and through that afternoon, the doctors debated where the bullet came in and went out. Perry said he assumed the smaller hole in Kennedy's neck was an entrance wound. They knew nothing of the events downtown, where some witnesses claimed a gunman by the infamous grassy knoll fired a shot from in front of the moving president. Lee Harvey Oswald fired from behind Kennedy as the limousine moved away from the book depository. At the time, the doctors hypothesized that perhaps a bullet entered at the front of the throat, ricocheted off the bony spinal column, and moved upward out the back of Kennedy's head. At that point, the doctors were unaware of the wound in Kennedy's back. McClelland stared at the hole in the back of the president's head. He looked at where the skull crumpled slightly around the edges. Knowing nothing else of the assassination at the time, he, too, assumed a bullet had come out of that opening.

He wouldn't feel confident in his initial assessment until eleven and half years later, when he and his wife watched an episode of *The Tonight Show* with Johnny Carson. As the couple got ready for bed, Carson introduced his guest, a young, ambitious television host named Geraldo Rivera. Rivera had with him footage of the assassination previously unseen by the public, footage known simply as "the Zapruder film." Shot by Abraham Zapruder, an immigrant from the Ukraine, the 8-millimeter Kodachrome movie shows the motorcade through the duration of the assassination. As McClelland watched it for the first time, he saw the back of the president's head blasted out. He saw the president swayed "back and to the left," a phrase later repeated ad nauseum in Oliver Stone's *JFK*. McClelland was convinced he had been standing over an exit wound.

WILLIAM KENNETH HORSLEY, MD

(from a letter from Horsley's wife, Donna)

Dr. William Kenneth Horsley was a senior medical student on that day and had vivid memories of what took place there when President Kennedy was brought in. Although he never talked about it very much, he was convinced by the wound that he saw that the fatal shot had come from in front of the president.

JOE D. GOLDSTRICH, MD

Kennedy wasn't breathing. The appearance of the neck wound is burned into my memory. It was a perfectly round hole between nickel and quarter size, in the middle of the front of the neck, just below the Adam's apple.

RON JONES, MD

(from *Baylor Reflections*)

President Lyndon Johnson established the Warren Commission on November 29, 1963. I was not contacted by the Warren Commission until the following spring—on Friday, March 20, 1964—although in the interim the Federal Bureau of Investigation did stop by at least once to interview me. My testimony for the Warren Commission was taken in Dallas by Counsel Arlen Specter, now a US senator. Questions were asked as to why I initially thought the neck wound was an entrance wound, whether I was a ballistics expert, and whether I had any notes other than those written the day following the assassination. It is interesting that I have seen my handwritten statement given to the commission stamped "top secret." I stated for the Warren Commission that the neck injury was very small and relatively clean, as you would see from a bullet that is entering rather than exiting a patient. If this were an exit wound, you would think that it exited at a very low velocity to produce no more damage than this had done, and if it was a missile of high velocity, I would expect more of an explosive type of exit wound, with more tissue destruction than appeared on examination. I had stated that I thought such a small throat wound could have been caused by a whole bullet only if it was traveling at an extremely low velocity, to the point that you might think that this bullet hardly made it through soft tissues.

JAMES CARRICO, MD

(oral history courtesy of the Sixth Floor Museum)

We were in our Saturday morning conference when the phone rang, and it was the pathologist in Bethesda, trying to get a hold of Dr. Malcolm Perry to get some medical information. And that was the first time, I think, that the pathologist in Bethesda knew that there was a wound here [pointing to center of neck] because all they saw apparently was a hole here [pointing to back right shoulder], a little hole here [pointing to back center of head], big hole here [right side of head], and a tracheotomy wound, and since they didn't have any medical records, they couldn't figure out how in the world three holes connected. So, they called Malcolm, and that's when they told him that these other two wounds were there, and that's when it kind of began to make sense that the bullet went in here [pointing to back of neck], came out here [pointing to center of neck], nicked his trachea, maybe hurt his spinal cord, but didn't kill him. The second bullet went in here [pointing to upper back portion of head], hit the bones inside his head, came out here [holding right side of head] and blew that big hole out. So, that was the first time we could really put things together in a way that made sense.

CHARLES BAXTER, MD

(excerpted from his testimony at the Warren Commission Hearings)

Mr. SPECTER. Will you describe with as much particularity as you can the wound which you noticed on the president's neck?

Dr. BAXTER. The wound on the neck was approximately an inch and a half above the manubrium of the sternum, the sternal notch. This wound was in my estimation, 4 to 5 mm. in widest diameter and was a spherical wound. The edges of it—the size of the wound is measured by the hole plus the damaged skin around the area, so that it was a very small wound. And, it was directly in the midline. Now, this wound was excised in the performance of the tracheotomy and on the entery [sic] into the deeper tissues of the neck, there was considerable contusion of the muscles of the anterior neck and a moderate amount of bleeding around the trachea. The trachea was deviated slightly, I believe, to the left.

Our tracheotomy incision was made in the second tracheal ring which was immediately above the area of damage—where we thought the damaged area of the trachea was, which we did not dissect out, but once the endotracheal tube was placed, the tracheotomy tube was placed into the trachea, it was below this tear in the trachea, and gave us good control or perfect control of respiration.

Mr. SPECTER. Were the characteristics of the wound on the neck sufficient to enable you to form an opinion with reasonable medical certainty as to what was the cause of the hole?

Dr. BAXTER. Well, the wound was, I think, compatible with a gunshot wound. It did not appear to be a jagged wound such as one would expect with a very high velocity rifle bullet. We could not determine, or did not determine at that time whether this represented an entry or an exit wound. Judging from the caliber of the rifle that we later found or become acquainted with, this would more resemble a wound of entry. However, due to the density of the tissues of the neck and depending upon what a bullet of such caliber would pass through, the tissues that it would pass through on the way to the neck, I think that the wound could well represent either exit or entry wound.

Mr. SPECTER. Assuming some factors in addition to those which you personally observed, Dr. Baxter, what would your opinion be if these additional facts were present: First, the President had a bullet wound of entry on the right posterior thorax just above the upper border of the scapula with the wound measuring 7 by 4 mm. in oval shape, being 14 cm. from the tip of the right acromion process and 14 cm. below the tip of the right mastoid process—assume this is the set of facts, that the wound just described was caused by a 6.5 mm. bullet shot from approximately 160 to 250 feet away from the President, from a weapon having a muzzle velocity of approximately 2,000 feet per second, assuming as a third factor that the bullet passed through the President's body, going in between the strap muscles of the shoulder without violating the pleura space and exited at a point in the midline of the neck, would the hole which you saw on the President's throat be consistent with an exit point, assuming the factors which I have just given to you?

Dr. BAXTER. Although it would be unusual for a high velocity missile of this type to cause a wound as you have described, the passage through tissue planes of this density could have well resulted in the sequence which you outline; namely, that the anterior wound does represent a wound of exit.

Mr. SPECTER. What would be the considerations which, in your mind, would make it, as you characterized it, unlikely?

Dr. BAXTER. It would be unlikely because the damage that the bullet would create would be—first its speed would create a shock wave which would damage a larger number of tissues, as in its path, it would tend to strike, or usually would strike, tissues of greater density than this particular missile did and would then begin to tumble and would create larger jagged—the further it went, the more jagged would be the damage that it created; so that ordinarily there would have been a rather large wound of exit.

Mr. SPECTER. But relating the situation as I hypothesized it for you?

Dr. BAXTER. Then it is perfectly understandable that this wound of exit was not of any greater magnitude than it was.

Mr. SPECTER. Dr. Baxter, is there a channel through which the bullet could have passed in the general direction which I have described to you where there would be very few tissues and virtually no tissues of great density?

Dr. BAXTER Yes; passing through the fascial plane which you have described, it could well not have these things happen to it, so that it would pass directly through—almost as if passing through a sheet of paper and the wound of exit would be no larger than the wound we saw.

Ron Jones, MD

(Oral history courtesy Sixth Floor Museum)

Editor's note: *What follows is the most remarkable revelation I came upon in researching this book. It appears that readily accessible accounts of the shooting were being ignored.*

So, you don't always know, and you're a little cautious as to who interviews you over the phone. If it's somebody who's really interested [smiling] and a civilian, or is it somebody that's trying to be somewhat sensational? I've had calls to participate in movies and BBC and so forth, but I was also directed as to what I was to say and describe the injuries in a little different fashion, such as maybe the president was shot in the temple instead of in the back of the head. And I refused to do that, and when I did, they had no more use for me. Now, Arlen Specter talked to me after the deposition outside the room in Parkland Hospital in the administrator's office, and he said . . . that was a fairly intense query that he did with me, and . . . but afterwards, he said in the hall—and this is in March of 1964—he said, "We have people who would testify that they saw somebody shoot the president from the front." From either . . . off the bridge, as I recall. I think there was a rail bridge in front of that street. "But we don't want to interview them, and I don't want you saying anything about that either. But we do have those people." And so, for years, I didn't say anything about that, and in retrospect, I think now it's pretty well known that there are people [smiling] who would testify to almost anything or that they saw this or saw that. But we were concerned about what we said and who would pick up on it at the—or at least, I was concerned about what I said—and who would pick up on it at the governmental level [nodding]. And maybe call you about that and inquire based on what you had testified and yet on what you might have said, but he said that right after the deposition.

KEMP CLARK, MD

(excerpted from his testimony at the Warren Commission Hearings)

Mr. SPECTER. What did Dr. Perry say at that time, during the course of that press conference, when the cameras were operating?

Dr. CLARK. As I recall, Dr. Perry stated that there was a small wound in the president's throat, that he made the incision for the tracheotomy through this wound. He discovered that the trachea was deviated so he felt that the missile had entered the president's chest. He asked for chest tubes then to be placed in the pleural cavities. He was asked if this wound in the throat was an entrance wound or an exit wound. He said it was small and clean so it could have been an entrance wound.

AFTERWORD

That's how we remember it, even if we all don't remember it the same way. I feel honored to have received the memories of forty-three doctors who have survived to tell the tale, and to have found the recorded recollections of those who have not. Their words seem to echo in the corridors of time. We were young when we bore witness to this tragedy, and, as in Longfellow's poem, "the thoughts of youth are long, long thoughts."

The final entry I received was from the still awesome Donald Seldin, who, at ninety-two, continues into his seventh decade of teaching at Southwestern. He was at his desk at the school when I called. So was his successor as Chairman of Medicine, the dear man Dan Foster. He's eighty-three and still teaching, as is Robert McClelland at age eighty-four. Are these guys going to outlive *all* of their students? Precious creatures, these.

Compressed into that hour on November 22 are memories as vivid as when our parents heard on the radio that Pearl Harbor had been reduced to a flaming inferno. The tragic moments we witnessed seemed to stop the world, and then leave it greatly changed thereafter.

It is said that the mastery of traumatic memory follows a course in which the trauma keeps intruding into consciousness until it is processed into less painful, less jagged, recollection. Curiously, highly pleasurable experiences keep intruding in the same way. By now we hope we have mastered the raw emotion of the time, but *when* am I going to stop tearing up when I see the images of those hours?

When we were kids, junior high school age, Walter Cronkite narrated a black and white TV series (black and white was all there was!) entitled *You Are There*. The great moments of history were dramatized, from the death of Socrates to the Salem witch trials. Episodes would end with the marvelous resonance of Cronkite's voice intoning, "What sort of day was it? A day like all days, filled with those events that alter and illuminate our times . . . and *you were there*." And indeed on such a day, Walter Cronkite told the world through a veil of tears that our president had died at Parkland Hospital.

What is history? On the surface, it's a simple enough question, but we must heed the warning of Carl Sagan that there is much in the nature of history we do not understand.

I started this project believing that there was one history of these events, only to find many, each observed and remembered reality different from the rest. They shared, however, the lightning bolt of grief felt 'round the world. Maybe that is the only accurate history of that heart-breaking time.

INDEX